India, Pakistan, and the Bomb

CONTEMPORARY ASIA IN THE WORLD

Contemporary Asia in the World

DAVID C. KANG AND VICTOR D. CHA, EDITORS

This series aims to address a gap in the public policy and scholarly discussion of Asia. It seeks to promote books and studies that are on the cutting edge of their respective disciplines or in the promotion of multidisciplinary or interdisciplinary research but that are also accessible to a wider readership. The editors seek to showcase the best scholarly and public policy arguments on Asia from any field, including politics, history, economics, and cultural studies.

Beyond the Final Score: The Politics of Sport in Asia, Victor D. Cha, 2008
The Power of the Internet in China: Citizen Activism Online, Guobin Yang, 2009
China and India: Prospects for Peace, Jonathan Holslag, 2010

India, Pakistan, and the Bomb

DEBATING NUCLEAR STABILITY IN SOUTH ASIA

Šumit Ganguly and S. Paul Kapur

Columbia University Press New York

Columbia University Press

Publishers Since 1893

New York   Chichester, West Sussex

Copyright © 2010 Columbia University Press

All rights reserved

Library of Congress Cataloging-in-Publication Data

Ganguly, Šumit.

India, Pakistan, and the bomb : debating nuclear stability in South Asia /

Šumit Ganguly and S. Paul Kapur.

p. cm. — (Contemporary Asia in the world)

Includes bibliographical references and index.

ISBN 978-0-231-14374-5 (cloth : alk. paper) — ISBN 978-0-231-51282-4 (ebook)

1. Nuclear arms control—India. 2. Nuclear arms control—Pakistan. 3. Nuclear

nonproliferation—India. 4. Nuclear nonproliferation—Pakistan. 5. Security,

International—India. 6. Security, International—Pakistan. 7. Indian—Foreign

relations—Pakistan. 8. Pakistan—Foreign relations—India. I. Kapur, S. Paul.

II. Title. III. Series.

JZ5665.G36 2010

327.1'7470954—dc22

2009030578

To the memory of my father, Romendranath Ganguly
—Šumit Ganguly

For I. L. K.
—S. Paul Kapur

Contents

Acknowledgments

Šumit Ganguly: I would like to acknowledge the thoughtful comments of Jack Snyder on an early version of this work. The usual caveats apply.

Anne Routon proved to be a most patient, supportive, and diligent editor.

Portions of the book appeared as "Nuclear Stability in South Asia," in the fall 2008 issue of *International Security*. I thank the Massachusetts Institute of Technology Press for permission to reuse that material here.

Paul Kapur is not merely a coauthor but a good friend, reliable colleague, and thoughtful critic.

ooooo

S. Paul Kapur: Anne Routon encouraged us to undertake this project and guided it expertly through the publication process.

Stanford University's Center for International Security and Cooperation provided me with an ideal intellectual environment while I worked on the manuscript. I thank Scott Sagan, Lynn Eden, and the rest of the center for their support.

Portions of the book appeared as "Ten Years of Instability in a Nuclear South Asia," in the fall 2008 issue of *International Security*. I thank the

Massachusetts Institute of Technology Press for permission to reuse that material here.

Jude Shell and Laura Thom provided excellent research assistance.

Šumit Ganguly was a first-rate intellectual opponent, outstanding colleague, and good friend throughout this project.

Finally, I am grateful to my family for their unflagging support.

The views that I express in this book are mine alone and not necessarily those of the Department of Defense.

Abbreviations

ballistic missile defense	BMD
Bharatiya Janata Party	BJP
Federally Administered Tribal Areas	FATA
gross domestic product	GDP
Indian Air Force	IAF
integrated battle groups	IBGs
Jaish-e-Mohammed	JeM
Jammu and Kashmir	J&K
Lashkar-e-Toiba	LeT
line of control	LOC
Northwest Frontier Province	NWFP
peaceful nuclear explosion	PNE
Students Islamic Movement of India	SIMI
Subterranean Nuclear Explosions Project	SNEP
Treaty on the Non-Proliferation of Nuclear Weapons	NPT

India, Pakistan, and the Bomb

1 | Introduction

India's and Pakistan's nuclear tests of May 1998 put to rest years of speculation as to whether the two countries, long suspected of developing covert weapons capabilities, would openly exercise their so-called nuclear option. The dust had hardly settled from the tests, however, when a firestorm of debate erupted over nuclear weapons' regional security implications. Optimistic observers argued that nuclearization would stabilize South Asia by making Indo-Pakistani conflict prohibitively risky. Pessimistic observers maintained that, given India and Pakistan's bitter historical rivalry, as well as the possibility of accident and miscalculation, proliferation would make the subcontinent more dangerous.[1] The tenth anniversary of the tests offered scholars an opportunity to revisit this issue with the benefit of a decade of hindsight. What lessons did the intervening years hold regarding nuclear weapons' impact on South Asian security?

Answering this question is important not simply from an academic standpoint; it has significant real-world implications. South Asia has emerged as a major player in international affairs, thanks in large part to its rapidly growing economy. India, which had been plagued by chronic underdevelopment for most of its history, has in recent years enjoyed GDP growth of approximately 8 percent. The country has become an important force in the information technology sector, a major source of skilled labor, and a burgeoning market for foreign exports.[2] In addition, South Asia's population is enormous. With well over 1 billion people between them, India and Pakistan account for more than one-fifth of the human race.[3] The subcontinent's conventional military power is also growing, with Indian capabilities in particular increasing rapidly.[4] Finally, South Asia has emerged as a region of central diplomatic importance. Indeed, the George W. Bush administration viewed improved relations with India as so important that it devised a deal to provide the Indians with civilian nuclear fuel and technology, despite India's refusal to sign the 1968 Treaty on the Non-Proliferation of Nuclear Weapons (NPT).[5] Pakistan, for its part, has been at the center of the global antiterrorism campaign since the attacks of September 11, 2001.[6] Developments in Pakistan will have especially serious implications for coalition efforts to rout the Taliban from Afghanistan and stabilize that country. Given these economic, demographic, strategic, and diplomatic factors, the international community has a significant stake in stability in the South Asian region.

Unfortunately, the subcontinent's history has been far from stable. Independent India and Pakistan emerged out of a bloody partition that left hundreds of thousands dead and millions displaced. The two countries then endured decades of hostility, including four wars and an ongoing conflict in Kashmir between Indian security forces and Pakistan-backed insurgents. Such a violent relationship, when combined with nuclear weapons, could prove to be a combustible mix. This danger makes proliferation's impact on the region an even more urgent subject for study.

Finally, South Asia's experience with nuclear weapons may offer lessons that are applicable well beyond the region. Current analyses of nuclear proliferation's likely effects are based largely on arguments drawn from Cold War history. But future proliferators such as North Korea or Iran may not closely resemble the United States or the Soviet Union. Indeed, they may have more in common with countries like India and Pakistan than with the two superpowers. If this is the case, then a careful study of nuclear weapons' impact on South Asia can help us anticipate their likely effects on future proliferators elsewhere around the globe. Although we do not explicitly discuss states such as Iran and North Korea, the basic principles underlying our arguments can be applied to them.

This book assesses nuclear weapons' impact on the South Asian security environment during three time periods: South Asia's nuclear past, spanning from the late 1980s through 2002; the nuclear present from 2002 through 2007; and the nuclear future, from 2008 forward. For the first two time periods, we attempt to determine the impact that nuclear weapons had on Indo-Pakistani relations and the strategic environment on the subcontinent. For the future, we speculate as to how past proliferation-related developments may affect the South Asian strategic environment in years to come.

Nuclear proliferation's impact on South Asia is the subject of a growing literature. In this book we take an approach that differs from existing works on the subject. First, we assess the issue of South Asian proliferation not from a single vantage point, but rather from two competing perspectives. Thus, although we examine the same historical evidence, we come to very different conclusions regarding nuclear weapons' impact on the subcontinent. Ganguly believes that nuclear weapons helped stabilize the regional security environment in the past; are to a large degree responsible for recent improvements in Indo-Pakistani strategic relations; and will help ensure that current improvements continue into the future. His argument is straightforward: Because nuclear weapons threaten to make conflict catastrophically costly, they induce caution in New Delhi and Islamabad. This has led the two sides to defuse ongoing crises without resorting to large-scale war and to take steps toward improving their larger strategic relationship. These factors have contributed to the current thaw in Indo-Pakistani relations and should continue to stabilize the subcontinent in coming years.

Kapur, in contrast, argues that nuclear weapons had a destabilizing effect on the South Asian security environment in the past; have little to do with recent improvements in Indo-Pakistani relations; and may destabilize South Asia in the future. Kapur maintains that nuclear weapons have had two negative effects on the South Asian security environment. First, nuclear weapons' ability to shield Pakistan against all-out Indian retaliation, and to attract international attention to Pakistan's dispute with India, encouraged aggressive Pakistani behavior. This, in turn, provoked forceful Indian responses, ranging from large-scale mobilization to limited war. Second, these Indo-Pakistani crises led India to adopt a more aggressive military posture toward Pakistan. This development could exacerbate regional security-dilemma dynamics and increase the likelihood of Indo-Pakistani conflict in years to come.

The second difference between this book and other works on the subject is that our arguments depart from standard optimist and pessimist offerings in the nuclear proliferation literature. Ganguly's argument shares rational deterrence theory's assumption that the potentially catastrophic costs of conflict promote stability in a nuclear environment. However, he differs from standard optimistic approaches in an important fashion. Virtually all the work on the stability of nuclear deterrence among horizontal proliferators is based on deductive logic and not detailed empirical analysis coupled with a theoretical corpus.[7] The most important work in this vein is that of Kenneth Waltz.[8] Two other important contributions, from Jordan Seng and from David J. Karl, while making compelling arguments about the viability of nuclear deterrence, are not based on careful examination of particular cases. Instead Seng relies mostly on carefully constructed arguments about the structure and disposition of small nuclear forces.[9] Karl, on the other hand, provides a modicum of empirical evidence from South Asia but bases his argument mostly on a critique of the propensity of nuclear pessimists to ascribe the baleful characteristics of the superpower experience with nuclear weapons to emerging nuclear powers.[10]

What distinguishes the present analysis from those of other proliferation optimists is the careful attention that it pays to the particular features of the South Asian political landscape. This work constitutes an attempt to carefully test the central premises of rational deterrence theory against a set of South Asian cases and demonstrate their robustness. In effect, the analysis moves away from largely logical and analytic exploration of the strategic consequences of proliferation and instead seeks to merge both theory and data.

Kapur offers a perspective that he calls strategic pessimism. This approach shares the pessimists' belief that the spread of nuclear weapons can be highly destabilizing. Unlike leading pessimist arguments, however, it does not locate proliferations' primary danger in suboptimal decision-making of the security and military organizations that control nuclear weapons. Rather, strategic pessimism shares optimists' assumption of rational decision-making on the part of new nuclear states and shows that wholly rational calculations may lead proliferators to adopt risky and destabilizing behavior.

We contextualize our competing positions, as well as the standard nuclear optimist and pessimist claims, as part of what we call outcome- and process-based approaches to nuclear proliferation. A key difference between optimistic and pessimistic arguments of all stripes is the emphasis they place on different aspects of crisis behavior. Optimists tend to stress the ultimately stable outcomes of past crises between nuclear powers, while pessimists focus on the potentially catastrophic processes by which the crises erupted and escalated. We argue that both sides make valid points; nuclear weapons may both encourage the outbreak of conflict and encourage states to ensure that violence remains limited. Whether the outcome- or process-based approach is ultimately superior depends on which aspect of crisis behavior one thinks is most significant.

Our approach has several important advantages. The book's debate-oriented structure, which alternates from point to counterpoint, gives the volume a conversational quality. This should make our analysis widely accessible while maintaining scholarly rigor. And it exposes the reader to competing sides of the South Asian proliferation argument in the space of a single volume. Our arguments, which differ in important ways from standard optimist and pessimist analyses, should add nuance to the nuclear proliferation debate.

ooooo

The book proceeds in the following manner. In chapter 2, we lay out the historical and theoretical background behind the current debate over South Asian nuclear proliferation. The chapter briefly traces the origins of the Indo-Pakistani conflict, outlines the history of the South Asian proliferation process, and locates disagreements within the policy and scholarly communities over nuclear weapons' effects on the region.

In chapter 3, we offer competing theoretical frameworks for understanding nuclear weapons' effects on Indo-Pakistani conflict behavior and on the behavior of new nuclear powers generally. In two contrasting sections, one by Ganguly and one by Kapur, we develop our arguments.

In chapter 4, we assess nuclear weapons' past impact on the South Asian security environment. The chapter examines the three major confrontations of the nuclear era—the 1990 standoff, the Kargil war, and the 2001–2002 standoff—according to the competing frameworks developed in chapter 3. Ganguly argues that nuclear weapons ensured that these crises did not escalate to the level of nuclear or full-scale conventional conflict. Kapur maintains that nuclear weapons facilitated the crises' outbreak and had little to do with their resolution.

In chapter 5, we address the current strategic environment in South Asia. Ganguly argues that by making continued conflict prohibitively dangerous, nuclear weapons have helped to promote the recent thaw in Indo-Pakistani relations. Kapur maintains that improvements in the regional security environment are modest and result more from economic, diplomatic, and domestic political factors than from nuclear deterrence.

We also look to South Asia's future. Ganguly predicts that the same deterrent logic that underlies recent improvements in the regional security environment is likely to continue to stabilize South Asia in the years to come. Despite acute crises in the region none of them have spiraled out of control and there appears to be little reason based on the available evidence to believe that they are likely to do so. Kapur claims that Indo-Pakistani conflict during the 1998–2002 period, which nuclear weapons facilitated, has led the Indians to begin formulating a more aggressive conventional military doctrine. This could increase Indo-Pakistani security competition and result in rapid escalation in the event of an actual conflict.

Finally, in chapter 6, we depart from our debate-oriented framework and discuss three issues about which we agree. First, we contextualize our competing arguments, as well as the standard nuclear optimist and pessimist claims, as part of what we call outcome- and process-based approaches to nuclear proliferation. Second, we argue against the potential introduction of ballistic missile defense capabilities into South Asia. Although BMD is billed as a defensive measure, in our view it would probably encourage arms racing and could even create first-strike incentives. Finally, we argue that nuclear weapons will be of little use in solving South Asia's most pressing security conundrum. Pakistan's decades-long support for anti-Indian militancy has created an array of terrorist organizations that Islamabad cannot fully control. They are wreaking havoc in both India and Pakistan, and could spark a catastrophic Indo-Pakistani confrontation. India and Pakistan's nuclear weapons will not enable them to eradicate this problem. The solution lies elsewhere, far outside the traditional boundaries of either side's security thinking. Pakistan will finally have to realize that the costs of supporting militancy outweigh its benefits, and end its support for insurgent organizations once and for all. India will have to continue its efforts to resolve tensions within Kashmir, address the legitimate grievances of its Muslim population, and start taking internal security matters far more seriously. Such non-nuclear strategies can help to make nuclear use in South Asia less likely.

2 | The History of Indo-Pakistani Conflict

The spread of nuclear weapons to South Asia has long been the subject of intense international concern. This concern has arisen from two major factors. First, India and Pakistan have a long, bloody history. The two countries were born out of a partition of British India in 1947. Muslims, Hindus, and Sikhs fled from those regions of the empire that would become parts of India and Pakistan. In the spate of Hindu-Muslim violence that followed, 500,000 to 1 million people were killed and roughly 15 million were displaced.[1] The bulk of this violence occurred in the state of Punjab.[2]

Partition left a legacy of animosity between India and Pakistan that continues to the present day.[3] And the division of the subcontinent gave rise to bitter territorial disputes that have festered for decades.[4] The conflict over control of the territory of Kashmir has been especially intractable, giving rise to four Indo-Pakistani wars as well as to a low-intensity conflict between Pakistani proxies and Indian security forces.[5] Kashmir continues to be the primary source of regional tension and would be the likely cause of any future Indo-Pakistani conflict.

The origins of the Kashmir dispute can be traced to the process of British colonial disengagement from the subcontinent. The two principal nationalist movements in British India, the Indian National Congress and the Muslim League, had failed to reach any accord on power sharing under the aegis of a united India. The League asserted that Congress, despite its espousal of the cause of secular nationalism, was unable to guarantee the rights of Muslims in a predominantly Hindu polity.[6] In the 1940s, the British made some belated efforts to preserve the unity of their subcontinental empire. However, when these attempts failed to meet the conflicting goals of the Congress and the League, the Crown chose to partition the subcontinent into the sovereign states of India and Pakistan.[7] Reflecting the ideology and beliefs of the League, predominantly Muslim regions in the northwest and northeast sections of British India became the foundation of the new Pakistani state.

Despite this arrangement, the British still confronted an important problem, namely the question of the future status of India's 562 "princely states."[8] These states had enjoyed nominal independence, recognizing the "paramount" status of the British and ceding control over defense, foreign affairs, and communications to the Crown. As independence approached, Lord Louis Mountbatten, India's last viceroy, decreed that the doctrine of paramountcy would lapse when the British left the subcontinent. Accordingly, the rulers of the princely states would have to decide whether to join India or Pakistan, based on their demographic composition and geographic propinquity. The vast majority of the states posed little problem. Their rulers recognized that they had no choice but to accept Lord Mountbatten's decree.

But the rulers of the states of Junagadh, Hyderabad, and Jammu and Kashmir refused to obey the viceroy. The nawab of Junagadh was Muslim; his subjects were predominantly Hindu; and his territory abutted the Indian province of Gujarat. Unwilling to accede to India, he fled to Pakistan with his family, after which Junagadh was absorbed into India. The Muslim nizam of Hyderabad, who ruled over a predominantly Hindu population, and whose territory lay deep inside the nascent Indian state, also proved to be recalcitrant. In the end, Hyderabad was incorporated into the Indian union by force.[9]

The state of Jammu and Kashmir posed a unique set of problems. Its monarch, Maharaja Hari Singh, was Hindu; his subjects were predominantly Muslim; and the state shared borders with both India and Pakistan.[10] The maharaja, loath to accede to either India or Pakistan, hoped to create an independent state. He was unwilling to join India because he correctly feared that New Delhi would strip him of the bulk of his privileges, especially his substantial landholdings. He was averse to joining Pakistan because he surmised that as a Hindu monarch who had done little to improve the lot of his Muslim subjects, he would fare poorly in a state created as the homeland for South Asian Muslims.[11] Consequently, almost two months after the independence of India and Pakistan, he still had not acceded to either state.

Hari Singh's vacillation, however, soon came to an end. In October 1947, a tribal rebellion broke out in Poonch, in the western reaches of Kashmir. Sensing an opportunity to exploit the situation, the government of Pakistan quickly entered the fray.[12] The Pakistanis sent in regular troops disguised as local tribesmen to aid the rebels. With Pakistani logistical, material, and organizational support, the rebels moved rapidly toward Srinagar, the summer capital of J&K, plundering and pillaging along the way. The maharaja's forces proved utterly incapable of stemming the onslaught.[13] Hari Singh, now in a state of panic, appealed to India for assistance. Prime Minister Nehru agreed to help, but only if two conditions were met. First, Kashmir would have to formally accede to India. Second, the Kashmiri people would have to approve the accession at a later date, once calm had been restored. Meanwhile, Nehru would accept the imprimatur of Sheikh Mohammed Abdullah, the leader of the Jammu and Kashmir National Conference, Kashmir's largest popular and secular political party. Only when he received Abdullah's explicit assent did Nehru proceed with accession.[14] Almost immediately, Indian troops were flown into Srinagar,[15] where they managed to stop the tribal advance, but not before the rebels had managed to seize about a third of the territory of the state.[16]

Despite periods of intense fighting, the situation on the ground changed little. Pakistan-backed forces, which included Hazara and Afridi tribesmen, paramilitary elements from organizations such as the Muslim League National Guards and regular Pakistan Army personnel had made quick work of Maharaja Hari Singh's troops. They then launched a three-pronged assault on a communications center located at Uri and damaged the power grid to Srinagar. On November 7, the Indian military counterattacked. They secured the Srinagar airfield, captured the town of Baramula, and by November 13 had managed to restore power to Srinagar.

These successes notwithstanding, by December the Indians were suffering from a paucity of logistical support and adequate high-altitude warfare equipment.[17] Pakistan-backed forces exploited this weakness, forcing an Indian retreat. Not until the spring of 1948 did the Indian forces managed to launch a counteroffensive. The Indian counteroffensive and its attendant territorial gains, however, resulted in more direct involvement by the Pakistan Army in Kashmir. And this, in turn, created further problems for the Indians. Pakistan Army parachute and artillery unit deployments, for example, threatened the slender communication links between Amritsar and the cities of Jammu, Pathankot, and Poonch in the state of Kashmir.[18]

As the fighting continued in this back-and-forth manner, Indian leaders concluded that the conflict would continue indefinitely unless they could devise a strategy to end Pakistani support for the Kashmiri rebels. To accomplish this end, India would have to dramatically expand the scope of the conflict. But the Indians realized they lacked the military resources to carry out such a strategy.[19] Cognizant of their military limitations, and acting on the advice of Lord Mountbatten, India referred the Kashmir question to the United Nations Security Council on January 1, 1948, where a diplomatic battle ensued.[20] On January 1, 1949, the UN imposed a cease-fire. At the time of the cease-fire, Pakistan was in possession of about one-third of the princely state and India the remaining two-thirds.

A second Indo-Pakistani war for Kashmir erupted sixteen years later. Its outbreak bore a striking similarity to the first Kashmir conflict. Pakistan again sought to seize the territory, using soldiers disguised as local inhabitants. A confluence of events—including internal political disturbances in Indian-controlled Kashmir in December 1963, the death of Prime Minister Nehru in 1964, the presence of a new and untested prime minister, Lal Bahadur Shastri, at the national helm, and India's willingness to refer a border dispute along the state of Gujarat to the International Court of Justice in May 1965—led the Pakistani military dictatorship of Ayub Khan to conclude that India would be unable to withstand a swift Pakistani onslaught. Based on this assumption, the Pakistanis forged a military strategy designed to seize the Indian-controlled portion of Kashmir. The plan had two distinct segments. The first was Operation Gibraltar and the second Operation Grand Slam. The initial segment involved sending lightly armed Pakistani troops disguised as locals into the Kashmir Valley. Once in the valley the troops were expected to link up with Pakistani sympathizers and foment a rebellion. Taking advantage of these disturbed conditions the Pakistan Army would then launch a full-scale assault on the valley, seizing it in a series of quick incursions. The plan, of course, was acutely dependent on the ability of the initial infiltrators and the local Pakistani sympathizers to wreak sufficient havoc and create conducive conditions for the invasion.[21]

The infiltration began along the 470-mile cease-fire line in Kashmir around August 5, 1965. The intruders carried small arms, hand grenades, plastic explosives, and radio equipment. Much to the dismay of the Pakistani military and political leadership, however, the local population did not support the infiltrators and instead turned them in to the authorities. Despite this loss of surprise, the Pakistanis decided to go ahead with their original war plans. They launched Operation Grand Slam on August 31–September 1 in southern Kashmir. Two infantry divisions spearheaded by seventy tanks constituted the Pakistani strike force. The Pakistanis hoped to capture the town of Akhnur, which would have enabled them to cut off the state of Jammu and Kashmir from the rest of India. In response, India escalated horizontally, launching a powerful attack directed against the Pakistani city of Lahore on September 6. Simultaneously, they also launched an offensive toward the town of Sialkot, a major nexus of roads and railways and a military center in the Punjab. These two coordinated offensives produced the desired result: They forced the Pakistanis to withdraw from Akhnur.

The Indian drive toward Lahore was initially quite successful, and the military managed to capture a number of villages along the way. In the end, however, the Indians were unable to assault Lahore directly, as the Pakistanis had destroyed the bridges across the Ichogil irrigation canal on the outskirts of the city. Similarly, the Indian effort to capture Sialkot failed in the wake of several inconclusive battles. Toward mid-September the war was reaching a stalemate. On September 20, the UN Security Council passed a unanimous resolution calling for a cease-fire.

India accepted the cease-fire resolution on September 21 and Pakistan on September 22. Under the Soviet-brokered Tashkent Agreement, which officially ended the 1965 war, both sides agreed in January 1966 to return to the status quo ante and to renounce the use of force in settling future disputes.[22]

One of the unanticipated outcomes of the 1965 Kashmir conflict was the growth of Bengali separatism in East Pakistan. The Pakistani military had long contended that the "defense of the east lay in the west" and so they chose not to deploy significant firepower in East Pakistan during the war. The Bengali population of East Pakistan realized that they had emerged mostly unscathed from the war thanks not to the Pakistani military, but rather to India's sufferance. Within less than a decade, their growing dissatisfaction with West Pakistani dominance would culminate in a civil war and contribute to the third Indio-Pakistani conflict, the 1971 Bangladesh war.[23] The Bangladesh war radically altered the region's territorial division and created the conventional military environment that has largely continued until today.

When Pakistan held its first national election in October 1970, the Bengali Awami League won a majority of seats in the National Assembly. But the League's demands for greater Bengali autonomy concerned Pakistani president Yahya Khan, who did not permit Awami League leader Mujibur Rehman to form a government. And Pakistan People's Party leader Zulfikar Ali Bhutto called for new elections, refusing to share power with Rehman. In response, large-scale rioting erupted in East Pakistan. West Pakistani troops, deployed to quash the violence, exacerbated the situation, slaughtering large numbers of intellectuals, Awami League members, and Hindus. Pakistan descended into civil war.[24]

These events unleashed a flood of refugees. Millions of East Pakistanis crossed the border into India to escape the violence, quickly exceeding India's capacity to absorb them. The Indians therefore sought to the stop the civil war by severing East and West Pakistan. To that end, in October and November, India began backing East Pakistani rebel forces, known as Mukti Bahini (literally "liberation force"). Pakistan retaliated on December 3 by launching air strikes against Indian air bases. This triggered a full-scale war. India attacked East Pakistan with six army divisions, rapidly penetrating East Pakistani territory. Although the Pakistanis hoped for assistance from friendly states such as the United States or China, none was forthcoming, and Pakistan was left to face India alone. The Indians made quick work of East Pakistan, capturing the capital of Dhaka by December 16 and declaring a cease-fire the next day.[25]

The consequences of Pakistan's loss were enormous. India had split Pakistan's Eastern and Western wings, capturing thousands of square miles of territory and tens of thousands of prisoners. India's overwhelming victory made clear that this was unlikely to happen in the future. Indeed, the Pakistanis would face the possibility of catastrophic defeat if they challenged the Indians again. This enhanced Indian confidence and undermined the Pakistanis' sense of martial superiority, cultivated over centuries of Muslim military dominance. The war also demonstrated that the Pakistanis could not depend on friendly states to ensure its survival. Finally, Pakistan's loss demonstrated that religion could not ensure state cohesion in South Asia. Ethnolinguistic differences had torn Pakistan asunder in 1971, despite the supposedly unifying force of Islam. Militarily, psychologically, diplomatically, and politically, Pakistan emerged from the Bangladesh war badly weakened.[26]

Indo-Pakistani relations became more stable following the Bangladesh conflict. Under the 1972 Simla Agreement, which reestablished diplomatic ties between the two countries following the war, India and Pakistan agreed to settle future disputes bilaterally and to respect the line of control separating Indian and Pakistani Kashmir. The Indians were satisfied with the post-Bangladesh settlement, which they believed would prevent the Pakistanis from involving outside parties such as the United Nations in the Kashmir dispute and from violently challenging Kashmir's territorial division. The Pakistanis, for their part, remained unhappy with territorial arrangements on the subcontinent. They continued to view the division of Kashmir as illegitimate and were smarting badly from the loss of their Eastern wing. However, they were not wholly dissatisfied with the Simla Agreement, which they interpreted quite differently from the Indians. The Pakistanis believed that, despite its emphasis on bilateralism, the agreement did not forbid them from referring the Kashmir dispute to third parties such as the United Nations. In addition, they believed that the language of the agreement did not foreclose future discussion of the Kashmir issue. Indeed, according to the Pakistanis, the agreement expressly envisioned India and Pakistan revisiting the Kashmir dispute at a later date. Thus the Pakistanis did not view Simla as being completely inimical to their interests.[27] Most importantly, following their crushing defeat in Bangladesh, the Pakistanis lacked the military wherewithal to challenge the Indians in Kashmir or elsewhere in the region. India and Pakistan did not fight another war for twenty-eight years.[28]

Despite the relative calm that prevailed in the wake of the Bangladesh war, Kashmir remained a serious, unresolved issue. Neither India nor Pakistan relinquished its claim to the territory. And over time the Kashmiri people became increasingly dissatisfied with Indian rule. During the 1965 war, Kashmiris were unwilling to take up arms against India, even when Pakistan offered them the opportunity to do so. But over the coming decades, Kashmiris' frustrations mounted, finally coming to a head with the outbreak of a violent insurgency in 1989.

The discontent resulted from a combination of political mobilization and institutional decay within Kashmir. The policies of both the Kashmiri National Conference and the Indian central government resulted in a proliferation of educational institutions, increased literacy rates, and greater access to mass media in Kashmir.[29] The Kashmiri population became far more politically sophisticated than it had been previously. Even as this was occurring, however, Kashmiri politics became increasingly deinstitutionalized, thereby reducing opportunities for legitimate political activity. In Kashmir, the National Conference monopolized power, preventing the emergence of any political opposition in the territory. And the Indian government dealt with Kashmir in an authoritarian manner, dismissing duly elected Kashmiri leaders, implementing heavy-handed antiterrorism laws, and centralizing power in New Delhi. When the National Conference conspired with the Indian government to fix the 1987 Kashmiri state assembly elections, Kashmiris were outraged, and the territory began its slide into violence. Demonstrations, strikes, and attacks against government targets erupted in 1988 and became more frequent in 1989. By 1990, Kashmir was in the throes of an all-out insurgency against Indian rule, forcing India to dissolve the Kashmiri state assembly and place the territory under governor's rule.[30]

The Kashmir insurgency was an indigenous phenomenon that resulted largely from Indian misrule in the region; Pakistan did not create the insurgency. The Pakistanis, however, were quick to take advantage of the opportunity that the Kashmiri uprising created for them. Pakistan began actively supporting the militancy, providing anti-Indian forces with training, arms, and infiltration and exfiltration across the line of control. This soon became a central element of Pakistani foreign policy and had a profound impact on the insurgency. It also inflicted substantial costs on India. The Pakistanis' strategy enabled them to threaten India's hold on Kashmir and attrit Indian resources. And it led India to implement draconian counterinsurgency measures that have damaged its international reputation. Approximately ninety thousand people have died in the insurgency, and despite recent improvements in the Kashmiri security situation, hundreds of thousands of Indian troops remain deployed in the region.[31] The Kashmir dispute had already given rise to periodic Indo-Pakistani conflicts. With the eruption of the insurgency, it also became an ongoing proxy war between India and Pakistan-backed forces.

The Indo-Pakistani relationship has thus been characterized by severe historical animosity dating from the founding of the two countries, numerous wars, and a festering territorial dispute that since the late 1980s has driven a low-intensity conflict between Indian forces and Pakistan-backed militants. Given this turbulent background, the international community found the notion of India and Pakistan acquiring nuclear weapons extremely worrisome.

The second reason for international concern over the possibility of nuclear proliferation in South Asia was that India and Pakistan pointedly refused to renounce their right to acquire nuclear weapons. During the 1960s, the United States, the Soviet Union, Britain, France, and China became deeply worried by the possibility that countries beyond their small group might acquire nuclear weapons. They created an international nonproliferation regime to prevent this from occurring. The centerpiece of the regime was the 1968 Non-Proliferation Treaty. The treaty forbade states from receiving, manufacturing, or seeking assistance in the manufacture of nuclear weapons or nuclear explosive devices.[32]

The NPT attracted a large number of signatories; by 2000, 187 states had acceded to the treaty. This included countries that were seriously considering the development of a nuclear weapons capacity but chose to abandon their ambitions and sign the NPT,[33] as well as states that had already developed nuclear weapons capabilities and decided to dismantle them in order to join the treaty.[34]

India and Pakistan, however, were among a small group of states that insisted on retaining their right to develop nuclear weapons and refused to sign the NPT. The two countries began actively pursuing nuclear programs soon after achieving independence. Despite Prime Minister Jawaharlal Nehru's public opposition to nuclear weapons, the Indian government established a Department of Atomic Research in 1954. India's crushing defeat in the 1962 Sino-Indian War, China's 1964 nuclear test, Chinese threats to intervene in the 1965 Indo-Pakistani War, and the existing nuclear powers' refusal to grant India a security guarantee, ultimately led the Indians to abandon their antinuclear posture. The Indians refused to sign the Nuclear Non-Proliferation Treaty, and they tested a nuclear device soon thereafter, achieving a fifteen-kiloton peaceful nuclear explosion (PNE) on May 18, 1974.[35]

Pakistan established its Atomic Energy Commission in 1957. Pakistani efforts initially focused on the production of civilian nuclear power. However, Pakistan's nuclear programs took on a military bent after the mid-1960s. Following the stalemated 1965 Indo-Pakistani war, the United States cut off arms transfers to Pakistan, and India began to achieve conventional superiority. Faced with this eroding military position, the Pakistanis refused to sign the Nuclear Non-Proliferation Treaty. Pakistan embarked on a full-fledged nuclear weapons program in 1972 after its devastating loss to India in the Bangladesh war.[36]

India and Pakistan's refusal to join the NPT and foreclose the possibility of acquiring nuclear weapons was not based solely on strategic calculations. Their position was also rooted in history. The two countries, previously ruled by Great Britain, had thrown off the colonial yoke only a few short decades before. Thus Indian and Pakistani leaders were loath to sign away their right to the security and status they believed nuclear weapons could bring them. They believed that Western efforts to prevent India and Pakistan from acquiring nuclear weapons resulted from a condescending, even racist, worldview. Indeed, Indian foreign minister Jaswant Singh famously labeled Western nonproliferation efforts "nuclear apartheid."[37]

Despite Western concerns, India and Pakistan pushed forward with their nuclear programs, and by the late 1980s the two countries were approaching a de facto nuclear weapons capability. Although neither country possessed a nuclear arsenal or had tested nuclear weapons, both India and Pakistan probably could have assembled nuclear devices in short order if the need to do so had arisen.[38] Some analysts believed that if such progress continued momentum toward testing and the development of overt nuclear arsenals would prove to be unstoppable.[39] Others argued that de facto nuclear capabilities afforded India and Pakistan robust deterrence; the knowledge that India and Pakistan could quickly assemble nuclear devices would make attacking them prohibitively dangerous and ensure their security. Thus, such analysts argued, India and Pakistan would have no need to test nuclear weapons and develop an overt nuclear capacity.[40]

The Indo-Pakistani nuclear tests brought these debates to an end. On May 11 and 13, 1998, India detonated five nuclear devices and the Pakistanis responded on May 28 and 30 with six nuclear explosions of their own. Clearly, de facto nuclear deterrence was insufficient to meet India and Pakistan's perceived political and security needs. Their governments wanted to ensure that their ability to inflict catastrophic damage on each other, or on any other adversary, was beyond question. Before long, however, a new controversy erupted over South Asian nuclear weapons. Now analysts argued over the impact that nuclear weapons capabilities were likely to have on the South Asian security environment. This discussion has been dominated by two main camps, labeled "proliferation optimists" and "proliferation pessimists." The optimist camp argues that the presence of nuclear weapons is likely to stabilize South Asia. Optimists believe that states' primary goal is to ensure their own survival and that states behave rationally, adopting policies designed to further their goals. Given these assumptions, optimistic scholars maintain that war between nuclear powers, which could result in the adversaries' annihilation, is highly unlikely. Thus, in the South Asian context, nuclear weapons greatly reduce the probability of Indo-Pakistani conflict, despite the two countries' antagonistic relationship. As Kenneth Waltz claims, both India and Pakistan "will be deterred [from aggression] by the knowledge that aggressive actions may lead to [their] own destruction."[41]

Pessimistic scholars argue that nuclear weapons will probably destabilize South Asia because of political, technological, and especially organizational factors. For example, the military services that control nuclear weapons may pursue their own bureaucratic and professional agendas while ignoring the larger interests of the state that they ostensibly serve. They may adopt offensive doctrines that appeal to military officers but can reduce crisis stability. Or they may employ safety procedures that are easily routinized but provide inadequate security for nuclear arsenals. Scott Sagan claims that "India and Pakistan face a dangerous nuclear future. . . . Imperfect humans inside imperfect organizations . . . will someday fail to produce secure nuclear deterrence."[42]

It is difficult to evaluate the relative merits of these positions. Scholars from the opposing camps have generally not grounded their work in the history and politics of South Asia. Indeed, they have explicitly downplayed the importance of such region-specific factors. For example, Waltz and Sagan believe that the behavior of new nuclear powers is likely to resemble that of the United States and the Soviet Union during the Cold War. According to Waltz, "Any state will be deterred by another's [nuclear] second-strike forces; one need not be preoccupied with the qualities of the state to be deterred. . . . In a nuclear world, any state— whether ruled by a Stalin, a Mao Zedong, a Saddam Hussein, or a Kim Jong Il—will be deterred by the knowledge that aggressive actions may lead to its own destruction."[43] Similarly, Sagan acknowledges that "there are differences" between Indo-Pakistani nuclear behavior and the nuclear relationship that developed between the United States and the USSR during the Cold War. India and Pakistan "will not make exactly the same mistakes as their superpower predecessors." However, he maintains that "while the differences are clear . . . the significance of these differences is not. . . . In both cases, the parochial interests and routine behaviors of the organizations that manage nuclear weapons limit the stability of nuclear deterrence."[44] Despite their differences, then, optimists and pessimists agree that proliferation's impact on the behavior of new nuclear states has little to do with the specifics of the proliferating states themselves.

As a result, competing arguments must be evaluated from a largely deductive standpoint. However, deductively speaking, optimistic and pessimistic approaches to nuclear weapons proliferation are equally plausible; there is no purely logical reason to believe that either deterrence-based or organizational arguments are more powerful. In order to judge the arguments' relative merits, one must carefully apply them to specific instances of nuclear proliferation and determine how well they explain observed phenomena. Does the behavior of nuclear proliferators in particular cases conform better to the expectations of the optimists or to those of the pessimists?

In the case of South Asia, a few recent works have taken such an approach, combining theoretical analysis with detailed, region-specific empirics. But these works have taken single positions in the proliferation debate; none of them have brought competing views together in a single volume, which would make it easier to compare their similarities and differences, and judge their relative strengths and weaknesses. In the pages that follow, we attempt to do so. Ganguly and Kapur offer opposing theoretical views of nuclear weapons proliferation, divergent descriptions of South Asia's nuclear past and present, and very different predictions regarding the region's nuclear future. In chapter 3, we discuss our opposing theories. Ganguly argues that nuclear weapons have contributed to stability in the region. By stability he means that neither side will now plan on carrying out a full-scale conventional war against the other for fear of nuclear escalation. Indian and Pakistani decision makers comprehend that nuclear weapons constitute a revolutionary breakthrough in warfare and see them solely as instruments of deterrence.

Kapur agrees that newly nuclear states should tend to behave rationally. He argues, however, that rationality is not enough to ensure stability in a nuclear environment. Indeed, nuclear weapons can create incentives for rational states to engage in highly destabilizing behavior. This, in Kapur's view, is precisely what has occurred in South Asia, making a nuclear subcontinent extremely dangerous.

3 | Competing Arguments About South Asian Proliferation

Nuclear weapons proliferation in South Asia has been a major international concern because of the region's violent history and because of India and Pakistan's refusal to accede to the international nonproliferation regime. The debate over South Asian proliferation shifted after 1998 from the question of whether India and Pakistan would acquire nuclear weapons to the question of what effects their nuclearization was likely to have on regional security. Two camps have dominated this post-test debate. The optimist camp argues that given nuclear weapons' ability to make any war between India and Pakistan catastrophically costly, nuclear proliferation should lower the likelihood of regional conflict. The pessimist camp argues that political, technological, and especially organizational pathologies will make proliferation dangerous, potentially leading to deterrence failure and war despite nuclear weapons' deterrent effects.

In this chapter, we offer our own views of nuclear weapons proliferation. Ganguly argues that nuclear weapons, contrary to much existing scholarship, can actually stabilize conflict-ridden relationships. Most nuclear pessimists underscore the dangers of organizational pathologies, and highlight the long history of Indo-Pakistani tensions and the existence of ongoing territorial disputes to argue that the introduction of nuclear weapons into the region would inevitably enhance the possibilities of conflict. These considerations, while seemingly compelling, are neither especially relevant to the South Asian context nor likely to render the region more war prone. Instead, careful examination shows that in the South Asian case, nuclear weapons have actually had quite a different effect. They have helped to stabilize an otherwise volatile region by making the potential costs of large-scale war unacceptably high.

Kapur offers a pessimistic argument regarding the effects of nuclear weapons proliferation in South Asia. Kapur's argument is not based on the organizational factors that dominate leading pessimist analyses of nuclear proliferation. He argues, rather, on rationalist grounds. Kapur's "strategic pessimism" maintains that states' relative military capabilities and territorial preferences can conspire to encourage destabilizing behavior on the part of new nuclear states. Specifically, states that are both weak relative to their principal adversary and dissatisfied with existing territorial arrangements may decide that they can challenge the territorial status quo without facing the danger of catastrophic defeat at the hands of their stronger adversary. And they may believe that ensuing nuclearized crises can attract international attention useful to their cause. Such behavior would occur not because of organizational or other pathologies, but because of states' rational calculation of their politico-military interests. Strategic pessimism thus challenges rational deterrence theory on its own ground showing how nuclear proliferation can increase the likelihood of risky behavior, crisis, and war, even between wholly rational states.

ŠUMIT GANGULY: THE OPTIMISTIC VIEW

A common set of problems afflicts most pessimistic analyses of the South Asian nuclear gyre. They tend to uncritically rely on deductive models and pay inadequate attention to the particular features of the political landscape of South Asia. As a consequence, these analyses, while theoretically sophisticated, have serious empirical shortcomings. For example, the organizational pathologies that Sagan identifies may well have been pertinent to the large, complex, and tightly coupled nuclear forces of the United States and the Soviet Union. But the nuclear forces of India and

Pakistan are small, are likely to remain so, and are not tightly coupled. Consequently, the organizational pathologies that afflicted the superpower relationship need not be replicated in South Asia.

Proliferation pessimists also highlight the war-proneness of military regimes because of the putative offensive bias of most military organizations.[1] Neither the Soviet Union nor the People's Republic of China was a military regime. However, they were regimes with professedly revolutionary ideologies and hardly averse to the use of force in international politics.[2] Nevertheless, they displayed exemplary restraint when involved in an acute international crisis. For example, the Soviet Union and the People's Republic of China were embroiled in a territorial dispute along the Ussuri River in the late 1960s. At that time, both states possessed nuclear arsenals, although the Chinese arsenal was in its incipient stages.[3] This territorial dispute erupted into war in March 1969 and resulted in considerable loss of life.[4] However, it did not escalate into full-scale war and the conflict was brought to a close through bilateral negotiations.

The Ussuri River clashes and their resolution demonstrate that two revolutionary states with risk-prone political leaderships can nevertheless exercise restraint and prevent the onset of a conflict spiral. More to the point, the Soviets who had significantly greater nuclear capabilities, chose not to carry out a preemptive strike on Chinese nuclear forces.[5] Admittedly, the Ussuri River conflict constitutes a single case. Nevertheless, it is emblematic of the restraint that was evinced in the midst of a significant border conflict. Consequently, it does not appear unreasonable to argue that similar restraint will ensue in the Indo-Pakistani context. Ultimately, minimally rational national leaders are, above all, interested in national survival. Consequently, they recognize the dramatic destructive powers of nuclear weapons and conclude that no possible political goal can be accomplished through their use, especially when their adversaries possess similar capabilities. Such a realization in turn induces substantial caution when in the midst of a crisis for fear of inadvertent or uncontrolled escalation to the nuclear level. Consequently, governments have every incentive to circumscribe the scope and dimensions of the conflict. In effect, this analysis reaffirms the central logic of rational deterrence theory: namely, that the sheer destructive potential of nuclear weapons forces even risk-prone decision makers to avoid provoking or coercing an adversary in a fashion that could induce it to consider resorting to the use of nuclear weapons.[6]

My argument's contribution, however, lies not in this deductive logic, which was pioneered in the work of Thomas Schelling and developed in that of Kenneth Waltz.[7] Instead its principal contribution lies in demonstrating that in this particular case the arguments of nuclear pessimists have been proven to be uniformly wanting. Decision makers in the South Asian region have come to fully grasp the awesome destructive power of nuclear weapons; they have learnt from repeated crises of the inherent dangers of an escalatory spiral and accordingly have taken fitful steps to try and reduce the nuclear danger in the region. Whether similar outcomes would obtain in other regions remains an open question. Leaders in other regions may prove to be more risk-prone; their military organizations may have a greater proclivity for the adoption of offensive doctrines; and their control over their weaponry may prove to be less robust.[8] Careful study of the South Asian case, however, suggests that these dangers are relatively low and so the robustness of nuclear deterrence is not at question.

SOUTH ASIA'S LONG PEACE

An important debate exists about the causes of the "long peace" that characterized Cold War Europe. The mutual possession of nuclear weapons and the horrific consequences of their possible use, according to one school of thought, can explain the long peace.[9] The other school contends that the explanation must be sought elsewhere. Its proponents believe that the terrifying memories of the two world wars effectively inoculated the population of the region to recoil from the prospect of a major war.[10]

The memories of war do not play a significant role in shaping the strategic behavior of political elites or mass publics in South Asia. All the Indo-Pakistani wars involved considerable mutual military restraint and produced relatively low levels of casualties.[11] However, in the South Asian context, the memories of the partition of the British Indian empire in 1947 have profoundly shaped the views of more than one generation of leaders in both states.[12] Specifically, Pakistan's rulers, both civilian and military, have harbored an irredentist claim to Kahsmir, the only Muslim-majority state in the Indian union. Even the successful secession of East Pakistan failed to undermine this claim. For Pakistan's leadership, Kashmir remains "the unfinished business of partition."[13]

Despite Pakistan's unwillingness to accept the territorial status quo in South Asia, there has been no major war in South Asia since 1971. Indeed, between 1971 and 1989, the region enjoyed its own period of long peace. This peace was based on overwhelming Indian conventional superiority and relative political quiescence in the disputed state of J&K.[14] Despite India's continuing military superiority, the onset of an indigenous ethnoreligious insurgency in December 1989 in Jammu and Kashmir contributed to renewed Indo-Pakistani tensions. Pakistan's decision makers, sensing an important opportunity to exploit India's self-inflicted wounds in Kashmir, devised a strategy to transform the insurgency into a well-funded, carefully orchestrated, religiously motivated extortion racket.[15] During this period, there was at least one major war scare, in 1990, as bellicose rhetoric on both sides over the question of Kashmir precipitated a crisis. Nevertheless, despite the stakes involved and the high level of ensuing tensions, war was successfully averted. The incipient nuclear capabilities of the two sides played a substantial role in preventing the outbreak of war.[16] By the end of the decade of the 1990s India had managed to restore a modicum of order, if not law in Kashmir. Indeed it can be argued that it was the very success of India's counterinsurgency strategy that promoted Pakistan's decision makers to pursue a "limited probe" in the Kargil region of Kashmir in 1999.[17] In this war the overt possession of nuclear weapons on both sides played a critical role in preventing an escalation or an expansion of the conflict.[18]

Thus Indian conventional superiority and the absence of any significant political turmoil within Kashmir ensured peace between 1971 and 1989. And after the outbreak of the insurgency, the incipient nuclear capabilities of the two sides induced considerable caution and prevented an outbreak of war despite a bloody, ongoing insurgency in Kashmir in which Pakistan became deeply involved. Multiple crises subsequently wreaked havoc in Indo-Pakistani relations since their mutual acquisition of nuclear weapons especially in 1999 and 2001–2002.[19] But despite intense tensions, none of these crises have culminated in full-scale war.

Decision makers in both countries have steadily and increasingly realized that the initiation of a major conventional conflict could, under a number of possible scenarios, tempt one side to consider the use of nuclear weapons. Consequently, both sides have exhibited considerable restraint and have chosen to eschew horizontal escalation and not to violate certain tacit thresholds.

Since the outbreak of the Kargil war, Indian military strategists have been struggling to forge a military doctrine and the requisite capabilities that might enable them to respond to future Pakistani provocation without triggering an escalation to full-scale war. It is far from clear that they will be able to formulate a viable doctrine that could effectively contain the possibilities of an escalatory spiral following the initiation of even limited attacks on Pakistani territory.[20] On the other hand, while Pakistan may deem the risks of abetting terror in India both controllable and calculable, it will also be loath to initiate a significant conventional conflict with India. Initiating a conventional conflict of such magnitude could invite substantial Indian retaliation and might push the two states toward a nuclear conflict.[21] Pakistan's decision makers may well be risk-prone; however, in their long history of conflict with India they have not engaged in fundamentally irrational behavior. They have been guilty of flawed judgment, have taken refuge in "false optimism," and have displayed strategic myopia.[22] None of these behavioral traits, however, are unique to Pakistani military and civilian officials.

Furthermore, there is evidence that the politico-military leadership does recognize the significance of the nuclear revolution and the unique properties of nuclear weapons.[23] Consequently, they are likely to see their nuclear capabilities as a viable deterrent against India's present and future conventional superiority. Barring a complete breakdown of the Pakistani state there is little reason to believe that nuclear deterrence will not remain robust in this bilateral relationship and help avert a full-scale war.

S. PAUL KAPUR: STRATEGIC PESSIMISM

The dominant school of proliferation pessimism argues that shortcomings within the organizations that manage nuclear weapons will make nuclear proliferation dangerous. For example, military services will adopt standard operating procedures that increase the likelihood of accident or will indulge officers' proclivity for offensive, destabilizing strategies. At first blush, this organizational argument appears to offer a fundamental challenge to the claims of proliferation optimism. Organizational pessimism expects proliferators to behave in ways that optimists do not predict, destabilizing rather than pacifying the international environment. Close examination reveals, however, that pessimist arguments in fact accept important optimistic beliefs. Specifically, pessimists do not challenge the optimists' claim that in a nuclear environment, strategic calculation should lead states to behave cautiously, thereby increasing international stability. Rather, pessimists show that organizational problems may short-circuit strategic policy formulation, preventing proliferators from adopting the cautious, stabilizing courses of action that they would otherwise embrace. Thus, in the leading pessimistic view, newly nuclear states will not behave dangerously because rational calculation or strategic policy formulation might encourage destabilizing behavior. Rather, dangerous behavior will occur because organizational pathologies interfere with strategic decision-making. Thus proliferation pessimism, in its dominant, organizational form, cedes important ground to the optimist camp. It does not challenge the optimists' fundamental claim that rational proliferators should be cautious proliferators

This is in no way to deny the significance of organizational pessimism's insights. Such pessimism points up important dangers that are likely to result from the spread of nuclear weapons. My claim is simply that despite its strengths the existing pessimist literature does not challenge proliferation optimism's core logic. In order to pose a more fundamental challenge to the optimists, a pessimistic approach would have to show that the acquisition of nuclear weapons could encourage destabilizing behavior even if states calculate rationally and behave strategically. I offer such an approach, arguing that even if they devise policy in a largely rational manner, newly nuclear states may decide not to behave cautiously. Instead, under certain circumstances, nuclear weapons can create strong incentives for rational states to adopt aggressive, extremely risky policies. Thus the spread of nuclear weapons can destabilize the international security environment even apart from the organizational logic that has so far driven the arguments of proliferation pessimists. In some cases, rational proliferators can be dangerous proliferators.

How could the acquisition of nuclear weapons create incentives for a state to behave in a destabilizing manner? Suppose that a state was dissatisfied with the location of its borders and militarily weak relative to its primary adversary. In this situation, the state's leaders would like to alter its territorial boundaries but would fear that doing so could trigger retaliation by the stronger adversary. Such retaliation could result in catastrophic defeat, involving a significant loss of territory or even of sovereignty. Thus the leaders of the weak, dissatisfied state would probably have to live with territorial boundaries that they viewed as undesirable.

Nuclear weapons would change this situation in two important ways. First, nuclear weapons would afford the weaker state a shield against its adversary's superior conventional military capabilities. If the strong state ever threatened the weak state with catastrophic military defeat, the weak state could respond with a nuclear attack. The strong state could still retaliate in the event of provocation by its weaker opponent. But the danger of a nuclear response would constrain the strong state, making it much less likely to launch a full-scale conventional attack against its adversary. This would not change the actual balance of power between the two sides. Nuclear danger, however, would limit the strong state's willingness to use its military capabilities. And thus nuclear weapons would nullify a good deal of the strong state's conventional military advantage. These developments could embolden the weak state to behave in ways that were previously too dangerous. Before acquiring nuclear weapons, the weak state had to fear that attempts to alter territorial boundaries might result in catastrophic defeat. Now, however, the weak state can directly challenge territorial boundaries, encouraged by the knowledge that its opponent is unlikely to employ the full extent of its military power in response.

Second, nuclear weapons could create diplomatic incentives for a weak, dissatisfied state to engage in destabilizing behavior. A nuclear conflict would have catastrophic human and economic effects;[24] it would also break the nuclear taboo in effect since the end of World War II.[25] The international community is extremely anxious to avoid a nuclear exchange anywhere in the world. Aggressive conventional military behavior that threatens to create a nuclear crisis can attract international attention, including mediation efforts by outside states. Such third-party intervention can result in a territorial settlement superior to any that the weak state could have secured in purely bilateral negotiations with its stronger adversary. Weak, dissatisfied states therefore may have a diplomatic incentive to engage in aggressive conventional military behavior that provokes their adversaries and creates a danger of nuclear confrontation.

It is important to note that proliferation is likely to be emboldening only where both of the criteria that I have specified are satisfied: The proliferating state must be territorially dissatisfied and militarily weak. If the state were satisfied with existing territorial boundaries, it would have no reason to attempt to change them, with or without nuclear weapons. And if the state were strong relative to its primary adversary, it would not need nuclear weapons to facilitate aggressive behavior. It could forcefully challenge existing boundaries even in a purely conventional military environment. Thus proliferation creates incentives for destabilizing behavior by weak, dissatisfied states, but not by those that are militarily strong, territorially satisfied, or both strong and satisfied.

Such provocative behavior by a newly nuclear state would be dangerous. It would invite forceful responses from the state's stronger adversary, which would seek to defeat ongoing aggression and to deter such behavior in the future. Even though neither side would wish resulting conflicts to spiral to the nuclear level, such escalation could occur. For example, the stronger state's retaliatory attack might be more successful than either state anticipated, quickly taking territory and threatening the weak state's nuclear command and control. In this situation, the weak state could delegate launch authority to field commanders or use its weapons before it lost the ability to do so.[26] This risk of inadvertent escalation would threaten to make even small-scale confrontations between new nuclear powers catastrophically costly.

Despite these dangers, however, aggressive behavior by a weak, dissatisfied proliferator would not be irrational. Nor would it necessarily be the result of organizational pathologies that short-circuited strategic decision-making. Rather, destabilizing behavior would be the product of a deliberate strategic calculation. A weak, dissatisfied proliferator would challenge existing territorial arrangements in the belief that its insulation from all-out retaliation, and its ability to attract international attention, would afford it a significant chance of achieving its politico-military goals. This means that nuclear weapons proliferation can be destabilizing quite apart from organizational or other pathologies. The structure of relative military capabilities and territorial preferences within a conflict relationship can also create strong incentives for dangerous behavior.

This is not to argue that all weak, dissatisfied proliferators will behave aggressively. The strength of incentives for aggressive behavior will depend to a large extent on a proliferator's level of dissatisfaction with existing territorial arrangements. The more dissatisfied a state is with current territorial boundaries, the more likely it is to attempt to change them by force. Thus a proliferator that is only mildly unhappy with existing arrangements may not behave aggressively. The level of a proliferator's relative military weakness will matter as well. A proliferator that is only slightly weaker than its adversary is less likely to need a shield against catastrophic defeat, and thus less likely to be emboldened by the acquisition of nuclear weapons, than a proliferator that suffers from a significant conventional military disparity. But despite these caveats, my basic point remains: Territorial dissatisfaction, conventional military weakness, and nuclear weapons are a potentially destabilizing combination.

I call my approach to nuclear weapons proliferation "strategic pessimism." Unlike standard organizational pessimism, it challenges the core logic of proliferation optimism, showing that the danger of nuclear weapons will not necessarily lead rationally calculating states to behave in a cautious manner. Instead, under the right circumstances, nuclear danger can create incentives for states to adopt aggressive strategies, thereby destabilizing ongoing conflict relationships and creating a serious risk of catastrophic escalation.

ooooo

In chapter 4, we apply our theories to Indo-Pakistani militarized disputes from the late 1980s through 2002. The increased number of militarized disputes during the early phase of nuclearization and even the overt acquisition of nuclear weapons, Ganguly contends, were inextricably related to the exigencies of regional politics. Nuclear weapons, far from exacerbating these tensions, actually helped to constrain and limit these crises. None of these crises were allowed to spiral into full-scale war despite high level of tensions and the significant stakes involved in them. The contrast with the prenuclear era could not be more dramatic. In the prenuclear era, both states made very deliberate (if not always careful) plans for war (see chapter 2). However, as both states came increasingly close to crossing the nuclear Rubicon they evinced a growing recognition of the dangers of nuclear escalation.

Kapur, on the other hand, maintains that strategic pessimism is best able to account for instability in South Asia after India and Pakistan's acquisition of nuclear weapons. As Pakistan developed a nuclear capability, its leaders decided that they could forcefully challenge territorial boundaries in Kashmir, the main source of Indo-Pakistani tension since partition. To this end they adopted policies ranging from the provision of extensive material support to the anti-Indian Kashmir insurgency, to the outright seizure of territory by the Pakistan Army. The Pakistanis believed that their nuclear capacity would prevent India from launching an all-out conventional attack in retaliation for these provocations. They also hoped that the danger of nuclear escalation in any ensuing crisis would attract international diplomatic intervention in the Kashmir dispute. India responded forcefully to Pakistani challenges, and the result was increased regional violence.

4 | South Asia's Nuclear Past

In chapter 3 we offer two competing views of nuclear weapons proliferation. Ganguly argues that nuclear weapons, far from destabilizing South Asia, actually constrained the prospect of major war in the region. He argues that the logic of nuclear deterrence, which had helped avoid major war among the great powers during the Cold War and had thereby contributed to the "long peace" in Europe, also holds in the South Asian context.[1] The sheer destructive properties of nuclear weapons ensures that decision makers act with a degree of caution and circumspection in the midst of international crises.

Kapur offers an approach to nuclear weapons proliferation that he calls strategic pessimism. Leading pessimistic arguments emphasize the danger of organizational pathologies, arguing that these problems will undermine states' ability to formulate rational security policies and to safely manage nuclear weapons. Strategic pessimism maintains that territorial preferences and conventional capabilities can create strong politico-military incentives for newly nuclear powers to behave aggressively. Thus nuclear proliferation can be dangerous and destabilizing based on states' rational calculation of their interests, quite apart from organizational shortcomings.

In this chapter, we discuss nuclear weapons' impact on Indo-Pakistani security relations from our competing theoretical viewpoints. We examine the period from the late 1980s, when India and Pakistan were beginning to acquire a de facto nuclear capability, through the Indo-Pakistani crisis of 2001–2002, when both countries were acknowledged nuclear powers. We seek to determine what, if any, impact nuclear weapons had on the outbreak, conduct, and resolution of regional crises during this period.

Ganguly claims that the crises did not originate in the gradual acquisition of nuclear arsenals on the part of India and Pakistan. Instead their origins can be located in the exigencies of Indian and Pakistani domestic politics. Despite significant domestic political upheavals in both states, Pakistan's propensity to exploit Indian domestic political discontent, and a series of concomitant crises, war was avoided in South Asia because both sides were acutely cognizant of the dangers of escalation. The mutual possession of even incipient nuclear capabilities actually helped deter war and also contributed to the swift conclusion of multiple crises. In the prenuclear era, neither side had evinced a propensity for restraint during confrontations.

Kapur maintains that nuclear weapons facilitated the outbreak of Indo-Pakistani militarized disputes during the years in question. Specifically, by shielding Pakistan from all-out Indian conventional retaliation and promising to draw international attention to the Kashmir dispute, nuclear weapons encouraged provocative Pakistani behavior. This ranged from the provision of extensive material support for anti-Indian militancy in Kashmir to outright seizure of Indian territory by Pakistani forces. India responded forcefully to Pakistani provocations, and this triggered a cycle of regional violence. Kapur argues that although the resulting Indo-Pakistani crises ended without large-scale conventional war or nuclear escalation, such fortunate outcomes had little to do with nuclear deterrence. Rather, conflict resolution resulted from nonnuclear factors, including conventional military constraints and diplomatic calculations.

THE LATE 1980s

Although India and Pakistan tested nuclear weapons and became open nuclear powers in 1998, the nuclear era in South Asia began well before that. India first detonated a nuclear device in 1974. This peaceful nuclear explosion had few military implications.[2] Nonetheless, the PNE demonstrated India's potential to develop a nuclear weapons capability in the relatively near future. Together with Pakistan's catastrophic loss of the 1971 Bangladesh war, the Indian test spurred the Pakistanis to energetically pursue their own nuclear weapons program.[3] Both sides continued to develop their capabilities in the years that followed, and by the late 1980s the two countries had managed to acquire a de facto nuclear weapons capacity. From roughly 1990 forward, India and Pakistan did not actually possess nuclear weapons but could probably have produced them in short order if necessary. As the years progressed, both sides increasingly viewed each other, and were seen by outside powers, as possessing a viable nuclear weapons capability.[4] Thus South Asia's nuclear era dates back not just to the 1998 tests, but to India's and Pakistan's acquisition of an untested and undeclared nuclear capacity at the end of the previous decade. What impact did the acquisition of a de facto nuclear weapons capacity have on the strategic environment in South Asia?

ŠUMIT GANGULY

India's nuclear weapons program originated shortly after its failure to obtain a nuclear guarantee from the great powers in the aftermath of the first Chinese nuclear test at Lop Nor in 1964.[5] In the aftermath of the rebuff from the great powers, India embarked on the Subterranean Nuclear Explosions Project (SNEP).[6] The SNEP culminated in India's first nuclear test in 1974.[7] Faced with widespread international disapprobation and substantial sanctions, the country curtailed the program. Prime Minister Morarji Desai, who briefly succeeded Prime Minister Indira Gandhi, was morally opposed to nuclear weapons and it is believed that he temporarily shelved the program. With Mrs. Gandhi's return to office, the program was revived. Fearful of external pressures, however, and cognizant of the fragility of India's domestic economic circumstances, she chose not to carry out further tests.[8]

During this time Pakistan steadily pursued a clandestine nuclear weapons program. The Pakistani program had its antecedents in the aftermath of the country's catastrophic defeat in the 1971 war.[9] Prime Minister Zulfikar Ali Bhutto had decided that only nuclear weapons could effectively counter Indian conventional superiority. It is difficult to pinpoint when exactly Pakistan managed to fabricate a full-fledged nuclear deterrent. However, long before the country is generally believed to have acquired such capabilities, it evinced no compunction in needling India when perceived opportunities arose. For example, in the early 1980s as a consequence of a confluence of domestic political forces, a major insurgency erupted in the Punjab.[10] Almost immediately, Pakistan entered the fray and contributed to its expansion.[11] Indeed, it was India's growing frustrations with Pakistani involvement in the Punjab that, in part, led India to embark on the Operation Brasstacks military exercise in 1987.[12] It was either during or immediately after this crisis that Pakistan acquired a viable nuclear weapons capability.[13]

The crisis that punctuated Indo-Pakistani relations in 1990 had little or nothing to do with Pakistan's possession of nuclear weapons. Instead it can be traced to the indigenous insurgency that erupted in the disputed state of J&K in December 1989.[14] As a consequence of their prior involvement in both the Punjab and Afghan insurgencies, Pakistani decision makers had come to an important strategic conclusion: Without paying a huge political or material price they could inflict dramatic costs on neighboring states through the use of proxy jihadi forces.[15] Not surprisingly, once the insurgency erupted, the Pakistani political leaders of Prime Minister Benazir Bhutto's party promptly entered the fray. The 1990 crisis, which marked one of the early peaks of the insurgency in the Indian-controlled part of the disputed state of Jammu and Kashmir, had little to do with nuclear weapons.

S. PAUL KAPUR

De facto nuclearization destabilized the South Asian security environment. It did so by emboldening the Pakistanis to pursue regional territorial goals that had previously been prohibitively dangerous. Pakistani leaders had been deeply unhappy with the division of Kashmir since India's partition in 1947 and had launched two wars with India over the territory. But Pakistan's crushing loss in the Bangladesh war clearly demonstrated that the Pakistanis could not risk fighting the Indians again. After 1972, the Pakistanis stopped challenging India for control of Kashmir. But they did not abandon the Kashmir cause. Rather, they reserved the right to fight for Kashmir later, when the strategic situation changed. As Zulfikar Ali Bhutto explained in the wake of the Bangladesh conflict: At present "I cannot go to war. Not in the next 5, 10 or 15 years." However, "if tomorrow the people of Kashmir start a freedom movement," Bhutto continued, "we will be with them. . . . We will fight if we want to fight. . . . This is an eternal position."[16]

By the late 1980s, Pakistan's strategic situation had in fact changed, enabling the Pakistanis once again to begin challenging the Kashmiri status quo. This change resulted from several factors. First, in 1989 an armed insurgency against Indian rule erupted in the territory of Jammu and Kashmir, killing large numbers of civilians and security personnel, and threatening to undermine Indian control of the region.[17] Second, the Afghan war offered a model that Pakistan could use to exploit the insurgency and defeat a stronger, occupying power in Kashmir. It also provided experienced military and intelligence personnel capable of executing such a strategy. In addition, the end of the war in Afghanistan freed large numbers of mujahideen from their battle with the Soviets, creating the possibility that these fighters could be redirected to wage jihad in Kashmir.[18] Third, Pakistani leaders believed that with the end of the Cold War, the world community might be more willing than it had been to address the Kashmir issue.[19]

But equally important as these factors was Pakistan's acquisition of a nuclear capacity, which would enable the Pakistanis to challenge territorial boundaries in Kashmir without fearing catastrophic Indian retaliation. Pakistani leaders openly acknowledge nuclear weapons' emboldening effect on their strategic calculations. Benazir Bhutto, who served her first term as Pakistani prime minister from 1988 to 1990, explains that Pakistan did not originally seek a nuclear capacity "for Kashmir-specific purposes." However, over time, the nuclear capacity's utility in Kashmir "came out" as a major factor in Pakistani strategic thinking. "Islamabad saw its capability as a deterrence to any future war with India [because] a conventional war could turn nuclear." India would not mount a large-scale conventional attack even in response to direct Pakistani provocations in Kashmir. "Irrespective of the presence of troops and the threat of war, India could not have launched a conventional war" against a nuclear-armed Pakistan. To do so would have been "suicide."[20]

Pakistani strategic analysts agree with this view. According to the Islamabad Institute of Strategic Studies' Shireen Mazari, for example, in a nuclear environment "each side knows it cannot cross a particular threshold." Thus "limited warfare in Kashmir becomes a viable option. At the very least, more material assistance can be given to the Kashmiri freedom fighters while Pakistan waits for the Indians to eventually come to the table for talks on Kashmir."[21] Even proliferation optimists admit that the Pakistanis' emerging nuclear capacity enabled them to adopt a more activist policy in Kashmir. Ganguly, for example, acknowledges that one of the "compelling reasons" why the Pakistani military was "emboldened . . . to aid the insurgency in Kashmir" in the late 1980s was that "they believed that their incipient nuclear capabilities had effectively neutralized whatever conventional military advantages India possessed."[22]

Pakistan's aggressive new policy in Kashmir led almost immediately to increased Indo-Pakistani tension. This was first demonstrated in a major militarized dispute that became known as the 1990 crisis.

THE 1990 CRISIS

The 1990 crisis arose primarily out of an Indian attempt to intimidate Pakistan and coerce it into ceasing its support for the Kashmir insurgency.[23] When the Kashmir insurgency erupted, India began augmenting its security forces in Kashmir and Punjab with regular-army infantry units, in hopes of stemming militant infiltrations from Pakistan and Azad Kashmir into Indian territory. In response, Pakistan deployed armored units into positions facing Indian Punjab and Rajasthan, and across the border from the road connecting Jammu to Punjab. In addition, forces from Pakistan's December 1989 Zarb-i-Momim military exercise, the largest in Pakistan's history, did not return to their peacetime stations; they lingered near the international border and the LOC in Kashmir. The Indians feared that these movements were designed to support terrorist operations within Indian territory. Meanwhile, in February, two Indian armored units deployed to a firing range in Rajasthan. The Pakistanis worried that these forces could form the nucleus of a large-scale Indian attack.[24]

This cycle of military action and reaction touched off a series of heated exchanges in the press between Indian and Pakistani leaders. In mid-March, Prime Minister Benazir Bhutto, during a visit to Pakistani Kashmir, announced the Pakistan was prepared for "one thousand years of war with Hindu India" in pursuit of Kashmiri freedom from Indian rule. Indian prime minister V. P. Singh, in an early April speech to the Lok Sabha, responded, "I warn them [that] those who talk about a thousand years of war should examine whether they will last [for] a thousand hours of war."[25]

By mid-April, roughly two hundred thousand army and paramilitary forces were deployed in Indian Kashmir, where they faced approximately a hundred thousand troops across the LOC in Pakistani Kashmir. Indian leaders feared that Pakistani forces could sever lines of communication between Punjab and Kashmir, and aid the Kashmiri insurgency. The Pakistanis, for their part, worried that India might launch a major armored thrust in Sindh or raid insurgent camps in Pakistani Kashmir.[26]

The unfolding events caught the attention of the U.S. government and in mid-May, U.S. deputy national security adviser Robert Gates traveled to Islamabad and New Delhi. Gates urged restraint on Pakistani and Indian leaders. He informed both sides that while India would likely win any full-scale Indo-Pakistani war, victory would be exceedingly costly. He secured a promise from Pakistani officials to close training camps for the Kashmiri insurgents and conveyed this news to the Indians. Gates also offered to provide India and Pakistan with satellite reconnaissance data to reassure each side that the other was withdrawing from its forward positions. The crisis deescalated soon after the Gates mission. India announced the return of its forward-deployed armor to its peacetime stations and proposed a number of confidence-building measures to Pakistan. Within two weeks of the Gates visit, the 1990 crisis was over.[27]

What, if any, impact did India and Pakistan's de facto nuclear capabilities have on the outbreak and resolution of the 1990 crisis?

ŠUMIT GANGULY

Nuclear pessimists often stress how close India and Pakistan came to nuclear war in 1990.[28] Whether they came close to war, let alone nuclear war, remains an open question. The fact remains, however, that despite rising tensions on both sides, war did not ensue. Contrary to pessimists' accounts, war did not occur because both sides were cognizant of the dangers of nuclear escalation. During this crisis both sides resorted to substantial military deployments but in the end chose not to resort to war. In all three possible theaters of conflict, Kashmir, Punjab, and Rajasthan, both sides had large troop and armor deployments. In Kashmir, in response to the insurgency and in an effort to secure the porous line of control, India had placed as many as two hundred thousand military and paramilitary forces in Kashmir. Pakistan, in turn, had deployed at least a hundred thousand troops. At some locations the troops were a mere tenth of a mile apart.[29]

Significant Indian and Pakistani deployments were also evident in the Punjab in frontline bunkers. Specifically, across the border from Lahore, the capital of Pakistani Punjab, India had deployed two infantry divisions.[30] The most dramatic Indian force deployments, however, were in the desert state of Rajasthan. India had brought to bear a three-division strike force, which included an armored division. A Pakistani corps based in Multan opposed this Indian formation. It is also believed that during this crisis Pakistan moved its nuclear weapons from a storage facility in Baluchistan to an air force base that had F-16 fighter aircraft modified to deliver nuclear ordnance.[31]

Despite these force movements and deployments and the high level of tension, the two sides averted war. How? More to the point, why? Why did India, which was facing a serious crisis in Kashmir significantly exacerbated by Pakistani involvement, refrain from launching a conventional attack on Pakistan? The answer indubitably must be attributed to their mutual possession of nuclear weapons. As General Krishnaswami Sundarji, a former chief of staff of the Indian Army, stated in a widely publicized interview, "Any sensible planner sitting on this side of the border is going to assume that Pakistan does indeed have a nuclear weapons capability. And by the same token, I rather suspect that the view from the other side is going to look very similar."[32]

Similar evidence about the role of nuclear weapons in preventing an outbreak of war can also be adduced from the Pakistani side. As a former chief of staff of the Pakistan Army, General Mirza Afzal Beg, stated in an interview, "We have no fear of war; [this lack of fear] has been possible because [of] nuclear deterrence which exists today on the subcontinent." Furthermore, he contended that "the fear of retaliation lessens the likelihood of war between India and Pakistan. I can assure you that if there was no such fear we would have probably gone to war in 1990."[33]

Finally, K. Subrahmanyam, India's noted strategic affairs analyst, made the most telling argument about the role of nuclear weapons in the 1990 crisis. As he wrote:

> The awareness on both sides of a nuclear capability that can enable either country to assemble nuclear weapons at short notice induces mutual caution. This caution is already evident on the part of India. In 1965 when Pakistan carried out Operation Gibraltar and sent in infiltrators, India sent its army across the cease-fire line to destroy the assembly points of the infiltrators. That escalated into a full-scale war. In 1990 when Pakistan once again carried out a massive infiltration of terrorists trained in Pakistan, India tried to deal with the problem on Indian territory and did not send its army into Pakistan-occupied Kashmir.[34]

To sum up the argument: despite substantial conventional military capabilities and significant pressure in the form of public opinion, India chose not to resort to military action against Pakistan during the 1990 crisis. Such restraint, as Subrahmanyam cogently argues, stemmed from India's knowledge of the existence of an incipient Pakistani nuclear weapons program.

S. PAUL KAPUR

Optimistic analysts believe that the 1990 crisis demonstrates nuclear weapons' pacifying effects on the South Asian security environment. Specifically, they argue that, in the absence of nuclear deterrence, India would most likely have attacked Pakistan and triggered a large-scale conflict in 1990.[35] In fact, multiple factors probably contributed to the standoff's peaceful resolution. Outside intervention such as the Gates mission may have helped.[36] Discussions between the Indian and Pakistani foreign ministers in the United States in late April may also have reduced tensions.[37]

But what of the optimists' claim that nuclear deterrence prevented an Indian attack during the 1990 crisis? Deterrence requires a potential aggressor to want to attack another party and to decide not to do so out of fear of costly retaliation. A state that did not actually wish to attack another cannot be said to have been deterred from doing so.[38] Close examination indicates that the Indian government never seriously considered attacking Pakistan during the 1990 crisis. The standoff's peaceful resolution therefore should not be attributed to Pakistani deterrence.

Even at the height of the 1990 crisis, it does not appear that India was undertaking any military action to prepare for a strike against Pakistan. Indeed, Indian and Pakistani deployments suggest a lack of hostile intent on the part of either party. In Kashmir, Punjab, and Rajasthan, India and Pakistan together possessed a total of four armored divisions. Only one Indian division, at the firing range in Rajasthan, was outside of its peacetime station, and no Indian or Pakistani units moved toward the international border during the crisis.[39] American military attachés in India and Pakistan had broad access to both sides' forces and did not view deployments during the crisis as being unusual or particularly provocative.[40]

Testimony from senior Indian military officers involved in the crisis supports this view. For example, Satish Nambiar, India's deputy director general of military operations in 1990, states that the "usual indicators of impending conflict, such as the dumping of ammunition and the laying of mines, were not seen" during the standoff. And since the Indian government did not want to take provocative actions "even in a cautionary manner," any aggressive "low-level moves at the command level were stopped by higher authority." Nambiar "never got the sense that the Indian political leadership wanted to escalate" the 1990 standoff.[41]

Senior Indian civilian officials hold similar views. For example, S. K. Singh, Indian foreign secretary during the crisis, characterizes the claim that India and Pakistan were on the brink of war in 1990 as "a fairy tale" and describes the standoff as "an elephantine non-crisis." According to

Singh, the idea of attacking Pakistan "did not cross anyone's mind in the Indian policy-making community anytime during those weeks."[42] Pakistani leaders evince similar views regarding Indian intentions. According to Benazir Bhutto, the Pakistan government did not believe that the Indians were planning to attack. "I believe the 1990 crisis was just overblown," she explains. "We never looked upon the threat as a serious threat from India. . . . It never was any danger point."[43]

Substantial evidence indicates that Indian leaders did not wish to strike Pakistan during the 1990 crisis. While this evidence does not prove that Pakistani nuclear weapons did not deter India from attacking Pakistan during the standoff, it strongly suggests that, as Chari, Cheema, and Cohen argue, "neither India nor Pakistan *wanted* to go to war in early 1990, despite the fact that the tension level between them had risen to an alarmingly high level."[44] Thus we should not consider Pakistani nuclear weapons to have deterred India from launching a war during the 1990 crisis.

Nuclear weapons did, however, play a significant role in triggering the 1990 crisis. The standoff arose out of India's attempt to force Pakistan to cease its support for separatists fighting Indian rule in Kashmir. The Pakistanis' willingness to provide the insurgency with extensive material support resulted to a great extent from the emboldening effects of its burgeoning nuclear capacity, which Pakistani leaders believed reduced the likelihood of large-scale Indian retaliation. In the absence of this capability, they probably would not have been willing to adopt such an aggressive policy in Kashmir. The 1990 crisis thus does not demonstrate nuclear weapons' stabilizing effects on the South Asian security environment. Rather, the standoff shows that nuclear weapons destabilized the subcontinent almost as soon as India and Pakistan began to acquire them.

ooooo

In the next section, we discuss nuclear weapons' effects on South Asia between 1998 and 2002. Ganguly argues that the 1999 Kargil crisis stemmed from a long-standing Pakistani plan to launch a "limited probe" and possibly present India with a fait accompli. The choice of the Kargil region was hardly accidental. Even though India could be expected to tenaciously defend against any incursion across the line of control, a Pakistani probe in this region did not threaten any fundamental Indian interests or military assets.

Kapur maintains that between 1998 and 2002 nuclear weapons continued to destabilize the region in much the same manner as they had previously. Indeed, in the wake of the 1998 nuclear tests, an overt nuclear weapons capacity emboldened the Pakistanis to behave even more provocatively than before, triggering the most serious Indo-Pakistani conflict in decades. This was soon followed by another major militarized standoff that brought the two sides to the brink of large-scale war.

NUCLEAR WEAPONS IN SOUTH ASIA, 1998–2002

In the years following the 1990 crisis, militant violence, supported by Pakistani arms, funds, and training, continued to wrack Indian Kashmir. Another large-scale Indo-Pakistani confrontation did not occur, however, until after the two countries' 1998 nuclear tests—an event that many observers expected would stabilize Indo-Pakistani relations.

At the time of the nuclear tests, India and Pakistan were enjoying a period of relative stability that had begun in the early 1970s. These years were not wholly tranquil and had been punctuated by periods of considerable tension. For example, a serious disagreement had arisen between the two countries during the mid-1980s over alleged Pakistani support for a Sikh separatist movement in the Indian Punjab.[45] Also, since 1989, India and Pakistan had been at loggerheads over the bloody insurgency against Indian rule in the state of Jammu and Kashmir. India accused Pakistan of materially assisting the Kashmiri separatists, while the Pakistanis maintained that they provided the rebels only political and moral support. Indo-Pakistani militarized disputes had become more frequent since the outbreak of the Kashmir uprising than they were during the 1970s and early to mid-1980s, and included the serious militarized crisis of 1990.[46] Nonetheless, despite these problems, the two countries had largely avoided serious confrontation during the nearly three decades since the Bangladesh war. Indeed, they had not fought a war with each other since 1972. This was the longest period without an Indo-Pakistani war since the two countries gained independence from Great Britain in 1947.[47]

In the wake of the 1998 tests, many observers believed that this relatively peaceful trend would continue. Yet less than a year after the tests, India and Pakistan were embroiled in their first war in twenty-eight years. In late 1998, Pakistan Army forces, disguised as local militants, crossed the line of control dividing Indian from Pakistani Kashmir and seized positions as much as seven miles inside Indian territory. The move threatened Indian lines of communication into northern Kashmir. After discovering the incursion in May, the Indians launched a spirited air and ground offensive to oust the intruders. The operation was characterized by intense, close-quarters combat, with Indian infantry and artillery ejecting the Pakistanis from the mountainous terrain peak by peak. Although expanding the war could have facilitated their task, the Indians did not cross the LOC, restricting their operations to the Indian side of the boundary. The Pakistanis finally withdrew in mid-July, after Prime Minister Nawaz Sharif traveled to Washington and signed an American-prepared agreement to restore the LOC. Over one thousand Indian and Pakistani forces died in the fighting.[48]

What impact did India and Pakistan's nuclear weapons capabilities have on the outbreak and resolution of the Kargil conflict?

ŠUMIT GANGULY

The origins of the Kargil conflict can be traced to Pakistan's interest in jump-starting the Kashmir insurgency. By the late 1990s, through a combination of political concessions and its counterinsurgency strategy, the Indian state had managed to restore a modicum of order if not law in Kashmir.[49] Furthermore, as a consequence of the restoration of some semblance of normalcy in the state, global attention on the Kashmir question was starting to wane. Under the circumstances, it was important for the Pakistani military to try and refocus international concern on the Kashmir question. To this end, the Pakistani military chose to make incursions in a region of Kashmir where none of India's vital security interests would be implicated.[50] If these incursions across the line of control proved successful, the Pakistani military would have been able to interdict one of the principal supply lines, National Highway 1A, to Indian troops on the disputed Siachen Glacier.[51] Such a military success would have significantly complicated India's logistical efforts to supply its troops on the glacier but would not have constituted a vital threat to its security interests.

Nevertheless, India mounted a concerted military operation to dislodge the Pakistani intruders. Though the Indian response was vigorous, it is important to note that the military were confronted with significant constraints on their actions. First, despite the availability of three strike corps, composed of sixty thousand soldiers broken down into three divisions each in the Punjab and Rajasthan, no orders were issued to open a second front.[52] Second, the Indian Air Force was used in offensive operations to dislodge carefully entrenched Pakistani forces along mountain redoubts. However, IAF personnel were issued strict orders not to cross the line of control under any circumstances. Even though this greatly hamstrung air offensive operations, the pilots scrupulously adhered to the political directive.[53]

India's extraordinary military restraint in this crisis constitutes an important puzzle. To begin with, the country's intelligence and security apparatus had been found seriously wanting.[54] More to the point, the principal political party in the ruling coalition, the Bharatiya Janata Party, was known for its bellicose views about Pakistan and its willingness to use force to settle international disputes. Despite its intransigence toward Pakistan, it had, in an effort to assuage global concerns about regional stability, undertaken a bold effort to try and reduce bilateral tensions a few months before the onset of the Kargil crisis.

Specifically, in February 1999, Prime Minister Atal Behari Vajpayee had opened a bus service linking the cities of Amritsar and Lahore and had traveled to Pakistan to work toward a possible Indo-Pakistan rapprochement. In considerable part, this gesture had been undertaken to assuage concerns on the part of the global community and to show that despite the nuclear tests, South Asia did not constitute a nuclear flashpoint.[55] His overture, at least notionally, had yielded significant results in the form of the Lahore Declaration. This statement called for a series of confidence-building measures and reaffirmed the stated resolve of both sides to seek a peaceful resolution of the Kashmir dispute.

Given that the Kargil incursions took place within three months of the Lahore Summit there was a profound sense of betrayal in New Delhi. Not surprisingly, passions ran high against the regime of Prime Minister Nawaz Sharif. An oncoming national election within a matter of months also placed substantial pressure on the BJP-led government in New Delhi to respond with decisiveness to the Pakistani incursions.

Despite the hostility of the BJP toward Pakistan, its profound sense of betrayal about the Lahore peace process, the significant reserve forces at hand, and electoral pressures, the regime kept the entire conflict limited in scope and dimensions. It refused to open a second front to alleviate pressures in Kashmir; it instructed the IAF not to carry out sorties across the line of control; and it sought to terminate the conflict as soon as the last intruders had been evicted from the Indian side of the LOC. It is hard to imagine that in the absence of Pakistan's possession of nuclear weapons India would have felt so constrained not to widen the scope of the conflict.

One possible objection to this line of argument needs to be anticipated and dealt with forthrightly. Did timely American intervention prevent an escalation of the conflict? This is a seemingly plausible and attractive explanation but it falls apart under careful scrutiny. Contrary to popular belief, the last major Indian military objective, the capture of Tiger Hill, took place a good *ten hours before* Prime Minister Nawaz Sharif met with President Bill Clinton on July 4, 1999, at Blair House in Washington, D.C. Sharif made this abrupt trip to Washington, D.C., in an attempt to elicit American assistance in terminating the conflict.[56] Though U.S. intercession did no harm, it cannot be adduced as a viable explanation for India's willingness to limit the scope of the conflict.[57] In effect, India had achieved its principal war aims before U.S.-Pakistani discussions to end Pakistan's incursions had started. American intercession may well have provided Prime Minister Nawaz Sharif the means for a face-saving retreat but it was not the critical element in ending the conflict.

S. PAUL KAPUR

The roots of the Kargil operation date back to the late 1980s, when Pakistan was beginning to acquire a nuclear capacity. Benazir Bhutto recalled that the army presented her with a Kargil-like plan in 1989 and 1996. According to Bhutto, the operation was designed to oust Indian forces from Siachen Glacier in northern Kashmir.[58] The army formulated a scheme by which Pakistani and Kashmiri forces would occupy the mountain peaks overlooking the Kargil region. The logic was that "if we scrambled up high enough . . . we could force India to withdraw" by severing their supply lines to Siachen. "To dislodge us," Bhutto recalled, the Indians "would have to resort to conventional war. However, our nuclear capability [gave] the military confidence that India [could not] wage a conventional war against Pakistan." Bhutto claimed that she rejected the proposal because even if it succeeded militarily, Pakistan lacked the political and diplomatic resources to achieve broader strategic success.[59]

Like these early plans, Pakistan's actual Kargil operation was designed primarily to threaten India's position in Siachen Glacier. According to Pakistani president Pervez Musharraf, "Kargil was fundamentally about Kashmir," where the Indians occupy Pakistani territory, "for example at Siachen. . . . Emotions run very high here" on this issue. "Siachen is barren wasteland, but it belongs to us."[60] Jalil Jilani, former director general for South Asia in Pakistan's Ministry of Foreign Affairs, describes Siachen as "perhaps the most important factor" underlying the Kargil operation. "Without Siachen," he argues, "Kargil would not have taken place."[61]

Again like the earlier plans, the actual Kargil operation was facilitated by Pakistan's nuclear capacity. But by 1999, thanks to the nuclear tests, the Pakistani capacity was overt. Whereas before skeptics might have questioned Pakistan's nuclear prowess, now no one could doubt it; Pakistan clearly possessed the ability to launch a nuclear retaliation in the event of a large-scale Indian conventional attack. Jilani explains that this overt capability increased Pakistani leaders' willingness to challenge India in Kashmir. In the absence of a clear Pakistani nuclear capacity, Jilani argues, "India wouldn't be restrained" in responding to such provocations. However, an overt Pakistani nuclear capability "brought about deterrence," ensuring that there would be "no major war" between India and Pakistan. In addition, conflict between two openly nuclear states would attract international attention, encouraging outside diplomatic intervention in Kashmir. Thus, as Jilani explained, nuclear weapons played a double role in Pakistani strategy at Kargil. They "deterred India" from all-out conventional retaliation against Pakistan. And they sent a message to the outside world regarding the importance of the Kashmir dispute. "War between nuclear powers is not a picnic. It's a very serious business. . . . One little incident in Kashmir could undermine everything."[62]

Pakistani analysts also note the emboldening impact of an overt nuclear capability on Pakistan's behavior in Kashmir. Shireen Mazari argues that "open testing makes a big difference in the robustness of deterrence," further encouraging the outbreak of limited warfare. "While this scenario was prevalent even when there was only a covert nuclear deterrence . . . overt nuclear capabilities . . . further accentuated this situation."[63] Proliferation optimists concede that these effects played a central role in facilitating the Kargil operation. Indeed, Ganguly argues that "overt nuclearization . . . bolstered [a] sense of false optimism" among Pakistani leaders. "Pakistani decision-makers had convinced themselves that their achievement of rough nuclear parity with India now enabled them to probe along the LOC with impunity. In their view, the Indian leadership, cognizant of Pakistan's nuclear capabilities, would decline to use overwhelming force and would also avoid a dramatic escalation or expansion of the conflict."[64] Elsewhere, Ganguly and Hagerty acknowledge that "absent nuclear weapons, Pakistan probably would not have undertaken the Kargil misadventure in the first place."[65]

Pakistani political leaders and strategic analysts, as well as optimistic South Asian security scholars, thus recognize nuclear weapons' emboldening impact on the Pakistanis' behavior in Kashmir and at Kargil. How, then, do scholars make an optimistic case for nuclear weapons' role in the Kargil conflict? Optimists argue that although nuclear weapons facilitated Kargil's outbreak, they also deterred India from crossing the LOC during the fighting, thereby ensuring that the dispute was resolved without resort to full-scale war. Thus Kargil shows that, on balance, nuclear weapons have not destabilized South Asia. Rather, optimists maintain, nuclear weapons' deterrent effects have prevented conflict escalation and thereby made the region safer.[66] Optimists are correct to argue that Indian leaders' refusal to cross the line of control prevented escalation of the Kargil conflict. However, Indian policy was not driven primarily by a fear of Pakistani nuclear weapons.

V. P. Malik, Indian Army chief of staff during Kargil, explains that the Indians avoided crossing the line of control mainly out of concern for world opinion. "The political leaders felt that India needed to make its case and get international support" for its position in the conflict. The Indian government believed that it could best do so by exercising restraint even in the face of clear Pakistani provocations.[67] G. Parthasarathy, India's high commissioner to Pakistan during the Kargil conflict, agrees. Indian leaders refrained from crossing the LOC, he explains, because they believed that doing so would yield "political gains with the world community." "We had to get the world to accept that this was Pakistan's fault." Staying on its side of the LOC enabled India to "keep the moral high ground."[68]

Despite these concerns, Indian leaders would probably have crossed the line of control if doing so had proved to be necessary. According to Malik, the civilian leadership's "overriding political goal . . . was to eject the intruders." The government made clear that it would revisit its policy if military leaders ever felt the need to cross the LOC. This did not occur because the Indians quickly began winning at Kargil and by early June were confident of victory. However, Malik maintains that "if the tactical situation had not gone well, India would have crossed the LOC," regardless of Pakistan's nuclear capacity. Pakistan had just shown that attacks across the line of control need not trigger nuclear escalation. Thus the Indians believed that Kargil could also be "done the other way."[69]

Former Indian national security adviser Brajesh Mishra offers a similar analysis. "The army never pushed the government to cross" the LOC, he explains. "If the army had wanted, the government would have considered crossing." Mishra maintains that Pakistan's nuclear capacity would not have deterred the cabinet from granting the army's request, since Pakistan would have been unlikely to use nuclear weapons in that scenario. "Pakistan can be finished by a few bombs," Mishra argues. "Anyone with a small degree of sanity would know that [nuclear war] would have disastrous consequences for Pakistan."[70]

Former defense minister George Fernandes supports these claims. According to Fernandes, India did not need to violate the line of control. Once the Indian counteroffensive got under way, the government was convinced that "India was in control [and] did not believe that the tactical situation was going to deteriorate." Simultaneously, the Pakistanis were suffering an international backlash, with "the United States . . . pressuring Pakistan" to undo the Kargil incursions.[71]

Former prime minister Atal Behari Vajpayee concurs with these assessments. "There was no need to cross the LOC," he explains, "because militarily India was successful. But nothing was ruled out. If ground realities had required military operations beyond the LOC, we would have seriously considered it. We never thought atomic weapons would be used, even if we had decided to cross the LOC."[72]

Tactical and diplomatic calculations, then, rather than Pakistani nuclear weapons, were primarily responsible for the Indian refusal to cross the LOC during the Kargil conflict. This does not mean that Pakistan's nuclear capacity was entirely irrelevant to Indian decision-making. Malik concedes that Pakistani nuclear weapons led the Indians to rule out full-scale conventional war with Pakistan. However, as he explains, nuclear weapons were "not decisive" in India's refusal to violate the LOC, since the Indians did not believe that crossing the line would trigger nuclear escalation.[73] Thus, nuclear weapons did have a limited stabilizing effect on the conduct of the Kargil conflict; the danger of a Pakistani nuclear response would have prevented India from deliberately launching a full-scale war against Pakistan. However, Pakistani nuclear deterrence did not prevent India from violating the line of control. Indian leaders' decision against crossing the LOC turned mainly on nonnuclear considerations.[74] And Pakistani nuclear weapons facilitated the outbreak of the Kargil conflict in the first place.

It is important to stress that although India and Pakistan managed to avoid both a nuclear and an all-out conventional confrontation at Kargil, such an outcome was hardly a foregone conclusion. Had the Indians not prevailed from behind the LOC, they probably would have crossed the line and escalated the conflict. We cannot know where such actions would have led. Although the Indians would not have deliberately threatened Pakistan with catastrophic defeat, the Pakistanis could have perceived rapid Indian conventional gains as an existential threat, particularly if they endangered Pakistan's nuclear command and control capabilities. The Pakistanis could have responded with a large-scale conventional or even a nuclear attack.[75] Kargil's relatively restrained outcome belies the conflict's considerable danger.

In the late 1990s, South Asia experienced its first war in twenty-eight years. Between December 2001 and October 2002, it experienced the largest ever Indo-Pakistani militarized standoff. The standoff's size made its potential consequences even greater than those of Kargil.

THE 2001–2002 CRISIS

Kargil had been militarily and politically damaging to Pakistan. The operation cost Pakistan hundreds of soldiers, tarnished its international reputation, resulted in heightened civil-military tension, and failed to alter the regional balance of power.[76] But Pakistan and its proxies did not abandon their provocative behavior in the war's aftermath. Militants continued to flow from Pakistani Kashmir across the line of control into Indian territory. There they launched a number of serious terrorist incidents, such as hijacking an Indian Airlines aircraft and taking it to Afghanistan, and launching an October 2001 attack outside the Jammu and Kashmir Assembly. The violence culminated on December 13, 2001, when terrorists assaulted the Indian Parliament in New Delhi while it was in session. Although no members were harmed, five Indian security personnel died in a gun battle before the terrorists were killed.[77]

The Indian government determined that two Pakistan-backed militant groups, Lashkar-e-Toiba and Jaish-e-Mohammed, had carried out the assault. The result was a major Indo-Pakistani militarized dispute known as the 2001–2002 crisis. The crisis proceeded in two phases. During the first phase, in the immediate aftermath of the assault on Parliament, India launched Operation Parakram, mobilizing five hundred thousand troops along the line of control and the international border. The Indians simultaneously demanded that Pakistan surrender twenty criminals believed to be located in Pakistan, renounce terrorism, shut down terrorist training camps in Pakistani territory, and stanch the flow of militant infiltration into J&K. If Pakistan did not comply, the Indians planned to strike terrorist camps and seize territory in Pakistani Kashmir. Pakistan responded with its own large-scale deployments, and soon roughly 1 million troops were facing each other across the LOC and international border.[78]

In January 2002, President Pervez Musharraf took two important steps toward deescalating the crisis. First, he outlawed Lashkar-e-Toiba and Jaish-e-Mohammed. Then, in a nationally televised speech on January 12, he pledged to prevent Pakistani territory from being used to foment terrorism in Kashmir. U.S. secretary of state Colin Powell, visiting New Delhi after stopping in Islamabad, subsequently assured Indian leaders that Musharraf was working to reduce terrorism and was actively contemplating the extradition of non-Pakistanis who were on India's list of twenty fugitives.[79] In the wake of Powell's visit, the Indians decided not to attack Pakistan.[80] However, Indian forces remained deployed along the LOC and international border.

The second phase of the 2001–2002 crisis erupted on May 14, 2002, when terrorists killed thirty-two people at an Indian army camp at Kaluchak in Jammu.[81] Outraged Indian leaders formulated a military response considerably more ambitious than the plans adopted in January. Now, rather than simply attacking across the LOC, the Indians planned to drive three strike corps from Rajasthan into Pakistan, engaging and destroying Pakistani forces and seizing territory in the Thar Desert. Before the Indians could act, however, the United States once again intervened. In early June, U.S. deputy secretary of state Richard Armitage extracted a promise from president Musharraf not just to reduce militant infiltration into Indian Kashmir, but to end infiltration "permanently." Armitage conveyed Musharraf's pledge to Indian officials, who subsequently decided not to attack Pakistan and to bring Operation Parakram to a close. Indian forces began withdrawing from the international border and LOC in October.

Why did India demobilize without attacking Pakistan? Did nuclear weapons play a role in persuading Indian leaders to back down during the 2001–2002 crisis?

ŠUMIT GANGULY

Repeated and timely American interventions throughout the course of this crisis are frequently cited as the principal reasons for the avoidance of war. A careful scrutiny of the record demonstrates that this argument is not entirely satisfactory. In the immediate aftermath of the attack on the Indian parliament on December 13, 2001, the United States acted with considerable alacrity to fend off any precipitate Indian actions against Pakistan.[82] A combination of American pressure and the unavailability of viable conventional strike options against Pakistan at short notice inhibited India from undertaking a quick attack against either Pakistan territory or Pakistan-controlled Kashmir. Nevertheless, India embarked on a process of general mobilization of its forces with the explicit goal of preparing for a major conventional confrontation with Pakistan. As India geared up its forces for a possible war, the United States exerted pressure on Pakistan to rein in the jihadi forces and continued to urge India to exercise restraint.[83] U.S. efforts appeared to produce the appropriate response from General Musharraf when he gave a speech on January 12 in which he explicitly stated that "Pakistan will not allow its territory to be used for any terrorist activity anywhere in the world."[84] In the aftermath of this speech, India was placed in an awkward position. It could ill afford to lash out militarily before Pakistan had the opportunity to move against the jihadi organizations. In the aftermath of General Musharraf's speech, it appeared that he would make a serious attempt to dismantle the jihadi infrastructure.[85] Within a week of that speech, the U.S. secretary of state Colin Powell publicly praised Pakistan's attempts to crack down on Islamist militants.[86]

Over the next several months, militancy in Kashmir did decline. Such a decline, however, was also seasonal. During the winter months, given the state of mountain passes, infiltration normally declines. Despite the lack of militant activity, Indian forces remained on alert in pursuit of a strategy of "coercive diplomacy" designed to sustain pressure on Pakistan to end its support for insurgency and terrorism.[87]

This lull in terrorist activity would prove to be temporary. On May 14, 2002, a group of terrorists struck an Indian army base in Kaluchak outside Srinagar in Indian-controlled Kashmir killing some thirty people including ten children of military personnel.[88] Anger against Pakistan, which had subsided somewhat, once again came to the fore and India contemplated retaliation.[89] India's failure to resort to force in the wake of this attack remains a critical puzzle. Admittedly, Pakistan's forces had been on alert since the Indian mobilization in January. But given the brazenness of this attack and the popular pressures on a jingoistic regime, its failure to resort to military action cannot be casually dismissed.[90] The critical factor that inhibited India from resorting to any form of military action was, even after the Kaluchak massacre, Pakistan's ability to threaten to escalate to the nuclear level.[91] As Praveen Swami, one of India's most informed journalists has written:

> In interviews with the author, two senior Indian officials involved with Operation Parakram claimed that the Vajpayee government had long been contemplating possible military responses to the post-1998 escalation of violence by Pakistan-based groups. The risk of nuclear escalation, the officials said, was important in shaping Indian policy responses. Vajpayee feared that a full-scale military response to Pakistan-backed terrorism could precipitate a wider conflagration. Although Vajpayee believed that the risk of nuclear war was small, he nonetheless saw no advantage in precipitating a crisis of which it might be an outcome.[92]

Swami's discussion once again underscores the critical role of nuclear weapons in preventing the state from resorting to war. The BJP-led regime had few compunctions about the use of force. However, faced with the possibility of nuclear escalation it was forced to exercise considerable self-restraint.

S. PAUL KAPUR

Because the 2001–2002 crisis did not escalate to the level of combat, optimistic scholars argue that it demonstrates the stabilizing effects of nuclear weapons on the subcontinent.[93] The truth, however, is more complicated than the optimists suggest. Nuclear weapons did not play a major role in dissuading Indian leaders from attacking Pakistan during the first phase of the crisis in January 2002. The Indian government's restraint during this period resulted primarily from the belief that its policy against Pakistan was succeeding. The Indians also feared that, having lost the advantage of strategic surprise, they would find the costs of a conventional confrontation with Pakistan excessively high.[94]

Pakistan's nuclear capability did play a role in stabilizing the second phase of the crisis, in May and June 2002. The existence of Pakistani nuclear weapons prevented the Indians from planning an all-out attack against Pakistan during this period. As former Indian army vice chief of staff V. K. Sood explains, "India could sever Punjab and Sindh with its conventional forces." However, "Pakistan would use nuclear weapons in that scenario." The Indians therefore sought "not to fight for real estate," but rather to "draw Pakistani forces into battle . . . and inflict damage from which Pakistan would take a long time to recover."[95] Thus Pakistani nuclear weapons did not prevent India from planning for a significant attack against Pakistan proper, but they did ensure that the attack's projected scope would be limited, so as not to threaten Pakistan with catastrophic defeat. Additional reasons for India's failure to attack Pakistan in mid-2002 were the loss of the element of surprise; concern with the costs of a large-scale Indo-Pakistani conflict, including the possibility of nuclear escalation; and a desire to avoid angering the United States by attacking America's key ally in the Afghan war.[96]

Most importantly, however, Indian officials decided not to attack Pakistan because they viewed the Parakram deployment as having been successful. No further terrorism on the scale of the Parliament attack had occurred during the crisis. And the Indians had secured a Pakistani pledge, backed by American promises, to prevent such violence in the future. Vajpayee explains that "America gave us the assurance that something [would] be done by Pakistan about cross-border terrorism. . . . America gave us a clear assurance. That was an important factor" in the Indian decision to demobilize.[97] Fernandes maintains that India had "no reason to attack." The Indians had "stayed mobilized to make the point that another [terrorist] attack would result in an immediate response. . . . No further attacks happened."[98] According to Mishra, Operation Parakram's "national goal was to curb terrorism emanating from Pakistan.

That national goal ... was achieved."[99] Thus nuclear weapons' role in limiting the 2001–2002 crisis is mixed. In one instance nuclear weapons had little effect, and in another they did help ameliorate the dispute, though they were not the principal stabilizing factor.

In evaluating nuclear weapons' impact on the 2001–2002 crisis, however, one must not overlook their role in fomenting the standoff. The Parakram confrontation resulted from India's large-scale mobilization and associated coercive diplomacy, which in turn was a reaction to an attack on the Indian parliament and an Indian army installation by Pakistan-backed Kashmiri terrorist groups. The Parliament and Kaluchak attacks were part of a broad pattern of Pakistani low-intensity conflict that was promoted by Pakistan's nuclear weapons capacity. Regardless of any stabilizing effects they may have had later in the 2001–2002 dispute, nuclear weapons played a central role in instigating the crisis in the first place.

Nuclear proliferation thus had a destabilizing effect on South Asia during the period from 1998 to 2002. By encouraging provocative Pakistani behavior and forceful Indian responses, nuclear weapons facilitated the outbreak of the first Indo-Pakistani war in twenty-eight years and the largest-ever South Asian militarized standoff. And although nuclear deterrence did inject a measure of caution into Indian decision-making, it was not critical to stabilizing either dispute. Rather, the Kargil war and the 2001–2002 crisis failed to escalate primarily as the result of India's concern with international opinion, faith in the success of its coercive diplomacy, and conventional military limitations.

CONCLUSION

This chapter examines Indo-Pakistani security relations from the initial stages of South Asia's de facto nuclearization in the late 1980s through the 2001–2002 crisis, when both India and Pakistan possessed overt nuclear capabilities. We seek to explain nuclear weapons' impact on the outbreak, conduct, and resolution of Indo-Pakistani crises in light of the theoretical arguments that we offer in chapter 3. Ganguly argues that despite acute political differences and significant tensions, both sides understood the logic of nuclear deterrence. Even though they were prepared to engage in acrimonious exchanges and emplace troops and armor along disputed borders, neither side evinced much propensity for military escalation. Such restraint could only be attributed to the presence of nuclear weapons. Kapur maintains that ongoing regional conflict was consistent with the expectations of strategic pessimism. Nuclear weapons' ability to insulate Pakistan from all-out Indian retaliation and to attract international attention to Indo-Pakistani crises facilitated Pakistani attempts to undermine territorial boundaries in Kashmir. India responded forcefully, and the result was a cycle of regional conflict. Thus nuclear weapons encouraged risky behavior based on India's and Pakistan's rational calculations of their politico-military interests.

ooooo

In chapter 5 we discuss the South Asian security environment from 2002 to the present. This period has witnessed an improvement in Indo-Pakistani relations, as evidenced by the commencement of a peace process, the adoption of a raft of confidence-building measures, and a reduction in regional militarized disputes. Ganguly attributes these developments in large part to the pacifying effects of nuclear deterrence. Kapur maintains that security improvements have been modest and that nuclear weapons were not responsible for them. Instead, economic factors, domestic political pressures, and nonnuclear strategic considerations underlie the recent thaw in Indo-Pakistani relations. Kapur argues further that nuclear weapons actually triggered ongoing strategic developments that could destabilize the subcontinent well into the future.

5 | South Asia's Nuclear Present and Future

In chapter 4, we discuss nuclear weapons' impact on the South Asian strategic environment from the late 1980s through 2002. According to Ganguly, Pakistan sought during this period to exploit various internal conflicts within India, especially those in the states of Punjab and Jammu and Kashmir. Though Pakistani adventurism contributed to regional tensions, war did not break out between the two antagonists. Nuclear weapons, most assuredly, did not contribute to these tensions and, in considerable measure, helped in preventing them from escalating into full-scale war. Even when a conflict did occur in 1999, the mutual possession of nuclear weapons played a crucial role in containing the scope and dimensions of the war. India did respond forcefully to the Pakistani Kargil intrusions in 1999 but scrupulously kept the conflict confined to the region where the initial incursions had occurred. Ganguly contends that in the absence of nuclear weapons the war would have broadened in scope and become more sanguinary.

Kapur argues that the years from the late 1980s through 2002 were consistent with the expectations of strategic pessimism. As Pakistan acquired a nuclear capability, it began a pattern of provocative behavior, ranging from large-scale support for the Kashmir insurgency to outright seizure of Indian territory. Pakistan used its burgeoning nuclear capacity as a shield against full-scale Indian retaliation and as a means of attracting international attention to the Kashmir dispute. Forceful Indian responses resulted in escalating regional violence.

In this chapter, we discuss nuclear weapons' effects on the current regional security environment and speculate as to their likely impact in the future. Indo-Pakistani relations have improved in recent years; India and Pakistan have pursued a peace process, and violence has declined in Kashmir. What explains these developments? Ganguly argues that India's resort to coercive diplomacy in the aftermath of the terrorist attacks on the Indian parliament, while not entirely successful in altering the calculus of Pakistani behavior, nevertheless induced a degree of restraint. On the other hand, despite Pakistani provocation, India too has been deterred from resorting to military options for fear of setting off an escalatory spiral to the nuclear level. Kapur maintains that recent improvements in Indo-Pakistani relations have been modest and are largely unconnected with nuclear weapons. Instead they are the result of economic, diplomatic, and nonnuclear strategic factors.

Ganguly and Kapur also differ in their expectations for the future. Ganguly foresees that India may yet devise a viable military strategy to address Pakistan-sponsored, low-level terror without provoking a larger conflict. Forging such a strategy has not proven to be easy because of the low threshold that Pakistan has publicly set for a resort to nuclear weapons in the event of a conventional conflict with India. Nevertheless, Indian military planners believe that they can carve out a space short of full-scale war within which they can retaliate against Pakistani provocations.[1] Kapur, however, fears that nuclear weapons' destabilizing effects on the past will have negative ramifications for years to come. In an effort to prevent continued Pakistani adventurism, Indian strategists are augmenting their military capabilities and devising a conventional doctrine that will enable India to attack Pakistan more quickly than before. This could make conflict more likely to occur, and to escalate rapidly, in the future.

NUCLEAR WEAPONS IN SOUTH ASIA, 2002–2008

Since the 2001–2002 crisis, South Asia has not experienced any large-scale militarized crises. India and Pakistan have begun a peace dialogue to resolve the Kashmir dispute. And the two sides have adopted a series of confidence-building measures, such as a cross-LOC cease-fire; the restoration of transportation and trade links between Indian and Pakistani Kashmir; steps to increase the security of nuclear weapons; and cooperation on cross-border criminal activity such as human trafficking, currency counterfeiting, and illegal immigration.[2] Violence in Kashmir has decreased. According to the Indian government, terrorist-related incidents declined by 22 percent from 2004 to 2005, with civilian deaths falling 21 percent and security personnel deaths falling 33 percent. In 2006, terrorist incidents declined an additional 16 percent, killing 30 percent fewer civilians and 20 percent fewer security forces than during the previous year.[3] This has enabled Indian forces to begin to adopt a less aggressive posture in the region. For example, in late 2007, the Indian government announced that its troops would withdraw from positions in private schools, hospitals, and houses that they had occupied during the Kashmir uprising.[4]

It is important to recognize that these improvements in Indo-Pakistani relations, though real, have been modest. For example, despite notable progress, the Kashmiri security situation remains tense. In 2006, 1,667 terrorist incidents killed a total of 540 civilians and security personnel. In an effort to maximize casualties, militants have increasingly attacked "soft" targets, such as minority groups, tourists, and migrant laborers. And estimated militant infiltration into Indian territory from Pakistani Kashmir has declined only 4 percent from 2005. Indian security forces report that infiltrators show signs of increased professionalization and are skilled at such tasks as breaching fences and negotiating other physical barriers.[5] As a result, Indian and Kashmiri officials have opposed significant reductions in troop levels, and hundreds of thousands of Indian security forces remain stationed in the region. "Although the incidents of violence and militancy are on the decline it is not wise to lower our guard," said Indian Kashmir chief minister Ghulam Nabi Azad. Azad stated that Indian force levels would be "automatically reduced" and "troops would go to the barracks once the situation was completely under control."[6] According to a senior Indian diplomat closely involved with the Kashmir peace process, "It is difficult to say" how much the Indo-Pakistani security environment has improved. "The Kashmir evidence is mixed. Cross-border [militant] traffic reports are not very positive."

Meanwhile, the militants have shifted their geographical focus and are "now coming through Bangladesh with the help of Pakistani agencies. There has been a change in tactics but not a change in attitude."[7] As Indian defense analyst Raj Chengappa puts it, "We are not in a hair-trigger environment anymore. But the situation is still serious."[8]

Even if they have been modest, however, improvements in Indo-Pakistani relations are important, lowering the likelihood that major conflict will erupt between the two countries. Why have these changes occurred? To what extent have they resulted from nuclear deterrence? And what impact are nuclear weapons likely to have on Indo-Pakistani security relations in the future?

ŠUMIT GANGULY

In the aftermath of the 2001–2002 crisis, relations between India and Pakistan remained strained. However, the levels of infiltration from Pakistan into Kashmir declined.[9] Did the drop in infiltration result from India's exercise of coercive diplomacy? To this we have no clear-cut answer. It is certainly possible to surmise that the economic costs that India's massive deployment of firepower during Operation Parakram imposed on Pakistan coupled with American pressure led the military regime of General Musharraf to reevaluate its strategy of promoting terror in Kashmir.[10]

Despite this drop in infiltration, relations between India and Pakistan remained strained. Indeed not until February 2004 did the two sides agree to start a "composite dialogue" to address a range of outstanding bilateral issues, including the Kashmir question. They included discussions on conventional and nuclear confidence-building measures, the Siachen Glacier dispute, the Wullar/Tulbul Navigation Project, terrorism and drug trafficking, and the expansion of commercial and economic contacts.[11] These discussions proceeded apace to 2008 and made progress in a number of areas. Nevertheless, there was little substantive progress on the vexed question of Kashmir.

What has caused the current cold peace in South Asia? Three factors can be identified. First, the military regime of General Musharraf, dependent on American largesse, was loath to initiate yet another crisis with India. Such a reckless endeavor could easily undermine the invaluable U.S.-Pakistan relationship. Second, India's willingness to resort to coercive diplomacy had exacted a significant material price on Pakistan.[12] Consequently, it would have been unwise to precipitate another crisis. Third and finally, the shift from a BJP-dominated regime to a Congress-led regime in 2004 opened up the possibility of a more conciliatory relationship. That said, this cold peace may not have ensued were it not for the restraint that nuclear weapons had induced in the 2001–2002 crisis. Though both sides had come perilously close to war during that protracted confrontation, in the end nuclear weapons had been a vital force for mutual, and especially Indian, restraint. Forging such a strategy has not proven to be easy because of the low threshold that Pakistan has publicly set for a resort to nuclear weapons in the event of a conventional conflict with India. Still, Indian military planners believe that it is possible to do so.

What does the future hold for Indo-Pakistani relations? What role are nuclear weapons likely to play in this relationship? The evolution of the relationship is likely to depend on several factors operating at global and regional levels. At a global level, critical choices on the part of the United States can have an important impact on the Indo-Pakistani relationship. If the United States continues with its policy of "dehyphenation" and treats India and Pakistan as distinct entities, it could play a salutary role in the region.[13] This policy will entail dealing with significantly different issues in the two states while working on some common concerns. In Pakistan, the United States should concentrate on bolstering the current and future civilian regimes, concomitantly reducing the overweening presence and role of the military and inducing it to eschew the pursuit of jihadi terror as an instrument of its security policy and direct its assistance toward the reform of Pakistan's social and economic sectors. In dealing with India, the United States should offer continuing support for the country's fitful efforts toward economic liberalization, urge it to improve the efficacy of its internal security apparatus, and encourage it to fashion social policies designed to reduce religious tensions. It should also support ongoing efforts toward Indo-Pakistani rapprochement on the fraught question of Kashmir. However, it should avoid the temptation, however well meaning, to insert itself as a broker in this dispute.[14] The "shadow of the past"—to reverse Robert Axelrod's proposition—looms large in India about the United States' role in resolving the Kashmir dispute.[15] Indian policymakers still recall the crude Anglo-American attempts to induce India to settle the Kashmir dispute on terms favorable to Pakistan in the wake of the disastrous Sino-Indian border war of 1962.[16]

At a regional level, much depends on the evolution of the existing political order in Pakistan. If democracy remains fledgling and anemic within Pakistan, the military is likely to undermine any imaginative moves toward the resolution of the Kashmir dispute. On the other hand a consolidation of democratic rule in Pakistan could provide the basis of a sustained dialogue with India and an eventual settlement of the dispute. Similarly, weak and fractious coalition regimes in India could also impede progress on the Kashmir question. This is especially true because any negotiations on Kashmir would involve discussions at two levels: bilateral and domestic.[17] Any regime in New Delhi would have to conduct complex negotiations with Pakistan. It would also have to pursue discussions with various disaffected parties within Indian-controlled Kashmir to ensure that they would not derail negotiations with Pakistan.

What would constitute a settlement of the Kashmir dispute? The precise contours of such a resolution are virtually impossible to delineate. However, it is possible to outline some general principles that might serve as useful guidelines for its settlement. First, it would require Pakistan to end its support for and involvement with a range of jihadi organizations. As long as the Pakistani state relies on this option no regime in India will be prone to making any meaningful concessions. Second, Pakistan will need to accept that there will not be significant changes in the territorial status quo. It has resorted to war with India on four occasions (1947–48, 1965, 1971, and 1999) and has used a strategy of asymmetric warfare since 1989 but to little effect. After fending off repeated Pakistani depredations with the expenditure of much blood and treasure over six decades, no regime in New Delhi is likely to make significant territorial adjustments.[18] Third and finally, India will have to fashion a new political compact with the disaffected segments of the Kashmiri populace. There is little question that Pakistan has played a significant role in stirring and sustaining discontent within Indian-controlled Kashmir.[19] But it is equally true that flawed Indian policies and political choices helped precipitate the ethnoreligious insurgency that has wracked the state since 1989.[20]

What role are nuclear weapons likely to play in the evolution of this relationship? They are likely to contain the prospects of full-scale war. Crises and tensions may yet characterize Indo-Pakistani relations as long as the Pakistani state remains unhappy with the territorial status quo in Kashmir. However, as multiple crises from 1987 onward have demonstrated, neither side has been willing to expand the scope of various conflicts. Despite the existence of strong domestic sentiments, the presence of a jingoistic political party at the helm of power, and the existence of substantial military capabilities, India chose not to expand the scope of the 1999 Kargil war. Furthermore, in the 2001–2002 crisis, despite grave provocation, India limited itself to the exercise of coercive diplomacy. In the aftermath of the horrific terrorist attacks of November 2008, when incontrovertible evidence linked the terrorists to Pakistan, India embarked on a diplomatic campaign to isolate the Pakistani state but eschewed any risky or provocative military maneuvers.[21] Just as nuclear weapons capped the escalatory process in all these crises, they are likely to do so in future confrontations.

S. PAUL KAPUR

A number of observers suggest that recent improvements in Kashmir, and in broader Indo-Pakistani relations, have resulted from the pacifying effects of nuclear deterrence. V. R. Raghavan, for example, argues that "a peace process with Pakistan on Kashmir has commenced and will continue. The conflict stabilization and the future resolution of the dispute could well be attributed to deterrence operating in the region."[22] In truth, however, improvements in Indo-Pakistani relations have not resulted primarily from nuclear deterrence. The Pakistanis reduced their support for anti-Indian militancy for three main reasons. First, in the wake of the September 11, 2001 terrorist attacks, the American government realized that Islamic terrorism was a global problem with direct implications for the United States' own security. The Americans also decided that they needed Pakistan to serve as a leading partner in their new anti-terror coalition. Thus, while the United States had previously turned a blind eye toward Pakistani support for militancy in South Asia, it was no longer willing to do so. In order to serve as an ally in the U.S. antiterror-ism effort—thereby avoiding the United States' wrath and enjoying its considerable financial largesse—the Pakistanis were obliged to reduce support for Islamic insurgents in Kashmir, in some cases going so far as to outlaw militant groups.[23]

Second, Pakistani cooperation with the United States alienated Islamic militant organizations, which branded Musharraf a traitor. These groups subsequently turned against the Pakistani government and attempted on multiple occasions to assassinate Musharraf.[24] This led the government to take further measures against the militants, as a matter of self-preservation.

Third, Pakistan's internal security situation has deteriorated badly, with militant groups challenging the central government for control in areas such as the Northwest Frontier Province and Federally Admin-istered Tribal Areas. The militants, in league with terror organizations such as al-Qaeda, have launched a wave of terrorist violence that has wreaked havoc not just on NWFP and FATA but also on major cities such as Karachi, Lahore, and Islamabad. Terrorist attacks on noncom-batant targets in Pakistan more than doubled between 2006 and 2007, and deaths from terrorist violence increased fourfold, with 1,335 people killed.[25] In response, Pakistan has deployed roughly 100,000 troops to the tribal areas, where they have so far been largely ineffectual in quashing the militants.[26] Islamabad views the situation as an existential threat to the Pakistani state, and the Gilani government announced that defeating the terrorists would be the top priority of its first hundred days in office.[27] This struggle against internal threats has diverted Pakistani attention and resources from the Kashmir conflict and impeded Pakistan's abil-ity to pursue its low-intensity conflict strategy against India. As Gur-meet Kanwal argues, Pakistan is "unable to fight simultaneously on three fronts—a proxy war against India, the Al-Qaeda-Taliban combine in its North West Frontier Province and vicious internal instability."[28] As a result, the Pakistanis have been forced to scale back their involvement in militant operations against Indian Kashmir. Pakistan's reduced support for anti-Indian militancy, then, is not primarily the product of nuclear deterrence. Rather, this policy shift resulted largely from changes in Pakistan's regional strategic environment and domestic security situation in the aftermath of September 11, 2001.[29]

The Indians, for their part, have pursued improved relations with Pakistan for two principal reasons, neither of which stems from nuclear deterrence. The first reason is economic. In the early 1990s, Indian leaders made a decision to radically alter the country's economic growth strategy. Previously, India had adhered to a socialist development model, emphasizing industrial regulation, import substitution, and central planning.[30] Prime Minister Narasimha Rao and Finance Minister Manmohan Singh rejected this approach. They largely abandoned India's commitment to "import-substituting industrialization" and its associated regulatory regime, moving instead to more market-oriented economic policies. Key aspects of their new strategy included structural adjustment, the reduction of tariffs and agricultural subsidies, the loosening of industrial regulations, and the trimming of India's enormous public sector.[31]

The immediate impetus for these changes was a critical foreign exchange shortage that rocked India in the wake of the First Gulf War.[32] However, Indian leaders realized that this crisis resulted from causes far more fundamental than the Gulf conflict. Deep, structural weaknesses in the Indian economy were to blame. Major changes would be necessary if India was not simply to deal with its immediate problems but also to achieve longer-term goals of reducing poverty, shedding its third world status, and joining the first rank of nations.[33] Rao and Singh thus used the Gulf War crisis to make far-reaching changes to India's economic strategy.

Since the implementation of the reforms, India's economic performance has been impressive. Its gross domestic product is now over $4 trillion (purchasing power parity), making the Indian economy the sixth largest in the world.[34] Indian GDP growth, no longer stuck at the "Hindu" rate of roughly 3 percent, jumped from 5.6 percent to 8.4 percent between 1990 and 2005, and reached 9 percent in 2007. Despite the global economic downturn, Indian growth is expected to continue at 4.8 to 5.5 percent from 2009 to 2010. India has also become a major player in the information technology sector and an important international source of skilled labor. Its rapidly growing middle class offers a potentially vast market for foreign imports. Indo-U.S. trade has skyrocketed from approximately $4.5 billion in 1988 to roughly $27 billion in 2005.[35]

Increased prosperity resulting from recent growth has led to rising economic aspirations on the part of the Indian electorate. Indians increasingly expect, as Raj Chengappa puts it, "better jobs, the American dream." And Indian leaders realize that continued growth is necessary if India is to make further progress in combating poverty, improving living conditions, and improving its international stature. Indeed, according to some estimates, at a growth rate of 8 percent per year, India can bring its poverty rate into the single digits within two decades.[36] Economic growth has become India's main national priority.[37]

However, despite recent improvements, India faces significant economic challenges that could undermine future growth. For example, massive inequality, which has long plagued Indian society, continues unabated. Paradoxically, Indian economic growth has exacerbated the phenomenon. As the World Bank points out, "In a marked departure from previous decades, reforms of the 1990s were accompanied by a visible increase in income inequality."[38] Perhaps the most glaring example of this problem is the growing urban-rural divide. India's economic boom has primarily benefited its cities, leaving out much of the countryside, which is home to roughly 70 percent of its population. In fact, approximately half of rural India has yet to access the electric power grid.[39] According to the Indian government, more than 20 percent of the population lives in poverty. And 46 percent of Indian children are malnourished, versus 35 percent in sub-Saharan Africa and just 8 percent in China.[40] Such severe inequality could lead not just to lagging growth but also to social unrest in disadvantaged regions and socioeconomic sectors.[41] As Prime Minister Manmohan Singh puts it, such "equity concerns . . . can do incalculable harm to the cohesion of our polity. We need therefore to focus our attention on this as a matter of high national priority."[42]

Other problems include the desperate state of India's public education system. Approximately 33 percent of children fail to complete five years of schooling, and about the same percentage of the population is illiterate.[43] India's physical infrastructure is also a shambles and badly in need of large-scale investment. The resulting lack of transportation facilities has damaged India's agricultural sector, which loses 30 to 40 percent of its produce to waste. Agricultural growth declined from 6 percent to 2.7 percent between 2006 and 2007. Analysts believe that the Indian government will need to spend roughly $150 billion per year, rather than the $30 billion that it has earmarked for yearly infrastructure expenditure, if the country is to sustain robust economic growth. India's natural environment is also increasingly under threat. The burning of fossil fuels and industrial production that are part and parcel of economic expansion are also damaging India's air and water. A recent Blacksmith Institute report listed two Indian cities in its top ten most polluted places in the world.[44] According to a report by the Chittaranjan National Cancer Institute, more than 46 percent of Delhi's population suffers impaired lung function due to air pollution.[45] Such widespread damage to public health can undermine productivity and impede further economic growth. Finally, despite extensive reforms, the Indian economy continues to labor under a stifling regulatory regime. According to the World Bank, in 2006, India ranked 134th out of 175 countries in ease of doing business.[46] Therefore, India might not continue its rapid economic growth. Expansion could stall if a large segment of its people remain malnourished and uneducated, its ports and roads are inadequate to move goods and services efficiently throughout the country, or punitive regulations impede wealth creation.

Indian economic growth, then, is not only extremely important to the country's future but is also potentially fragile. As a result, New Delhi hopes to avoid continued Indo-Pakistani conflict. More strife with Pakistan would be a significant distraction, diverting precious political and financial resources from the task of ensuring continued expansion. Also, Indo-Pakistani conflict could damage India's budding trade relationships, particularly with the United States. Conflict with Pakistan could damage India's international image and put India in the awkward position of fighting with a major U.S. ally. The resulting harm to Indo-U.S. relations could be financially costly and pose a further threat to continued Indian growth.[47]

The Indian government wishes to create, as Indian foreign secretary Shivshankar Menon put it, a "peaceful and prosperous periphery. . . . Without a peaceful and prosperous neighborhood, we cannot concentrate upon the urgent task of improving the lives of our people through continued and rapid social and economic development. It therefore follows that good-neighborly relations with Pakistan, or at least normalized relations and a modus vivendi, are in India's interest."[48]

The second major factor underlying India's pursuit of improved relations with Pakistan is the nature of anti-Indian terrorism. Pakistan-backed terrorists continue to launch bloody attacks on targets in the Indian heartland. For example, in October 2005, a series of bombings in New Delhi street markets killed approximately 60 people on the eve of the Hindu festival of Diwali. And in July 2006, a spate of bombings killed approximately 180 people on commuter trains and in railway stations in Mumbai. Indian authorities blamed the Pakistan-backed Lashkar-e-Toiba and Jaish-e-Mohammed, as well as the Students Islamic Movement of India, for the attacks.[49] However, despite apparent Pakistani involvement and the large number of casualties, the Diwali and Mumbai blasts were less of a national affront than the Parliament and Kaluchak attacks, which targeted the foremost symbol of the Indian state and the family members of Indian military personnel.

New Delhi has therefore opted for restraint despite ongoing terrorist violence. For example, after the Diwali attacks, Prime Minister Manmohan Singh urged citizens to "remain calm, not to panic or believe rumors and ensure that we go about our normal activities."[50] And after the Mumbai blasts, the prime minister again exhorted Indians "to remain calm. Do not be provoked by rumors. Do not let anyone divide us. Our strength lies in our unity. Let us stand together as one people, as one nation."[51] The government resisted calls for a more forceful response, which were widespread at the time. For example, after the Diwali bombings, the *Times of India* argued that India should "send out a hard-hitting, unambiguous message: that we are not willing to accept such outrages as part of our fate. . . . This is no time to be genteel and 'civilised' in our response. It's time we got angry."[52] According to the *Pioneer*, "By calling for restraint and asking people not to get carried away, the prime minister and his men mock at the memory of those who perished . . . or have been maimed for the rest of their lives."[53]

The Indian government did condemn cross-border involvement in the attacks and promised to defeat the terrorists. But the government's focus was primarily on domestic security measures, rather than on military action or on coercive threats aimed at Pakistan. In the wake of the Mumbai bombings, for instance, Prime Minister Singh highlighted the need to "upgrade our technological capabilities, our electronic surveillance systems, our communication interception capabilities, our access control systems to vital installations and high profile targets, . . . [to] improve ground level intelligence, [and] to have rapid response plans to ensure effective management" after a terror attack "and quick restoration of normalcy."[54] The Indians took no rhetorical or military steps to threaten to attack Pakistan as they did during the 2001–2002 crisis.

If a provocation on the scale of the Parliament attack were to occur in the future, however, the outcome might be very different. India might well launch a major militarized response against Pakistan, regardless of Pakistani nuclear weapons.[55] Indeed, the political pressure to do so could be overwhelming. As one prominent Indian strategic analyst puts it, "In the event of another major terrorist attack there will be an uproar and it will be politically impossible for the government not to respond."[56] In addition, Indian leaders continue to believe, as they did during the Kargil conflict and the 2001–2002 crisis, that they can engage Pakistan in large-scale conventional combat without starting a nuclear war.[57] Thus the Indian government's domestic and military calculations could create strong incentives for severe retaliation.[58]

As with Pakistan, then, India's pursuit of improved Indo-Pakistani relations has not resulted from nuclear deterrence. Rather, it is the product primarily of shifting domestic priorities and nonnuclear strategic calculations. And the Indian government's political will to continue its rapprochement with Pakistan could dissolve in the event of another Parliament-like terrorist assault. In fact, Indian strategists are actively preparing for the possibility of such an occurrence. These preparations may significantly affect the balance of power in the South Asian region and could exacerbate regional security-dilemma dynamics, increasing the likelihood of conflict. Thus nuclear weapons have had little to do with the current Indo-Pakistani rapprochement. In fact, by facilitating past disputes, nuclear weapons have unleashed strategic developments that may destabilize South Asia well into the future.

NUCLEAR WEAPONS AND FUTURE INSTABILITY Nuclear weapons facilitated provocative behavior as Pakistan acquired a de facto nuclear capability in the 1980s, encouraging Pakistan to provide the Kashmir insurgency with extensive political and material support. And nuclear weapons promoted further Pakistani adventurism in the wake of the 1998 tests, thereby triggering major Indo-Pakistani crises such as the Kargil war and the 2001–2002 standoff. Significantly, the effect of these crises has not been limited to the past. They have had a profound effect on current Indian strategic thinking, inspiring an aggressive shift in India's conventional military posture. This shift could increase the likelihood of serious Indo-Pakistani conflict in years to come.

The emerging strategic dangers are twofold. First, India is in the process of significantly expanding its conventional military capabilities. From 2001 to 2006, the Indian defense budget increased by 60 percent, from $13.81 billion to $22.1 billion. Between 2007 and 2012 India is forecast to spend up to $40 billion solely on weapons procurement, including fighter aircraft, artillery, submarines, armor, and an aircraft carrier.[59] Indian officials hope that this push to modernize Indian military forces will see an increase in defense spending from roughly 2 to about 3 percent of the GDP.[60]

These plans for Indian military expansion are not directed solely at Pakistan, or at any other country. To a significant degree, they result from India's continued economic growth. India's impressive expansion has created an enormous need for energy. India is currently the fifth largest energy consumer in the world and is forecast to take the number 3 position, passing Russia and Japan, by 2030.[61] Experts estimate that in order to sustain its current levels of economic growth, Indian energy consumption will have to increase by approximately 4 percent per year. Oil satisfies approximately 30 percent of Indian energy needs, and more than 60 percent of India's oil is imported.[62] As economic expansion continues, India must secure an increasingly global energy lifeline. This task will require India to project power across oceans into the Middle East and Southeast Asia. And such a power projection mission will require significantly increased military capabilities, particularly in the naval sphere.[63] Thus higher defense spending and a larger, more capable Indian arsenal is inexorably linked to India's continued economic growth.

But even if increased defense capabilities are the necessary result of India's growing economy, Indian planners also believe that a more capable force will enable them to inflict severe costs on Pakistan in the event of future conflict and potentially deter the Pakistanis from further adventurism. Thus India's military buildup is to an important degree aimed at Pakistan and has resulted directly from recent Pakistani provocations. As Indian defense writer Sandeep Unnithan argues, "If Kargil and Parakram had not happened, there would be no [Indian] military modernization, since there would be no sense of urgency. Kargil and Parakram ended Indian complacency vis-à-vis Pakistan."[64]

Motivations aside, however, India's increased military spending cannot help but threaten Pakistan. Since its founding, Pakistan has been deeply insecure relative to India. At independence, Pakistan received 23 percent of British India's landmass and 18 percent of its population. The Pakistan Army was allocated six armored regiments, against India's fourteen; eight artillery regiments, against India's forty; and eight infantry regiments, against India's twenty-one. Pakistan also suffered from serious geographical challenges. For example, the country's Eastern and Western wings were separated by approximately one thousand miles of Indian territory. They also lacked strategic depth, making them vulnerable to deep penetration by Indian armor and mechanized infantry. And the Pakistan Army suffered from a severe shortage of officers, forcing it to rely heavily on British personnel.[65] Thus the Pakistani state began life facing severe military challenges. This contributed to an overriding focus on national security among Pakistani elites, which in turn promoted both the rise of Islamism and the ascendancy of the army in Pakistani politics.[66]

Since independence, Pakistan's security situation has of course improved. Nonetheless, Pakistan remains significantly weaker than India. For example, in 2008, India enjoyed a roughly 2:1 advantage in active duty personnel, and a 1.6:1 advantage in combat-capable aircraft and main battle tanks. India's defense budget was more than five times that of Pakistan.[67] And Pakistan continues to suffer from a lack of strategic depth. Augmented Indian military capabilities will, therefore, put further pressure on an already vulnerable Pakistan.

Traditionally, Pakistan's military weakness vis-à-vis India was mitigated by India's peacetime deployment of offensive forces deep in the interior of the country, far from the Indo-Pakistani border. As a result of this positioning, Indian forces were slow to mobilize against the Pakistanis, requiring several weeks before launching a large-scale offensive.[68] This gave Pakistan time to prepare its defenses and ward off any impending Indian attack. It also allowed the international community to bring diplomatic pressure to bear on India's civilian leadership, thereby preventing it from launching military action.

Many Indian military leaders believe that this mobilization problem prevented India from acting decisively during the 2001–2002 crisis. By the time Indian forces were prepared to move against Pakistan, the Pakistanis were able to ready their defenses, thereby making a potential Indian attack far more costly. Most importantly, the Indians' slowness enabled the United States to pressure the Indian government, convincing it to abandon plans to strike Pakistan. Thus, in the words of Sandeep Unnithan, Parakram demonstrated that India's "mobilization strategy was completely flawed."[69] In addition, the government's restraint caused rancor within the armed forces. Senior officers believed that civilian leaders misused the military, ordering it to undertake a long and costly deployment and then opting for retreat, leaving the Pakistanis unpunished. As a senior American defense official stationed in New Delhi puts it, Indian commanders "were frustrated. . . . They really wanted to go after Pakistan but couldn't."[70]

In order to prevent a recurrence of Parakram's failures, the Indians began to formulate a new Cold Start military doctrine, which will enable India to launch a large-scale offensive against Pakistan within seventy-two to ninety-six hours of a mobilization order. The doctrine will augment the offensive capabilities of India's traditionally defensive holding formations located close to the Indo-Pakistani border. It will also eventually shift offensive strike corps from their current locations in the Indian hinterland to bases closer to Pakistan. In the event of conflict, Cold Start would drive three to five division-size integrated battle groups (IBGs)—consisting of armor, mechanized infantry, and artillery—twelve to fifty miles into Pakistan along the length of the international border. The IBGs would aggressively engage Pakistani forces and seize a long, shallow swath of Pakistani territory. Cold Start would seek to achieve three goals: inflict significant attrition on enemy forces; retain Pakistani territory for use as a postconflict bargaining chip; and, by limiting the depth of Indian incursions, avoid triggering a Pakistani strategic nuclear response. Indian military planners hope these doctrinal changes, coupled with India's growing conventional military capabilities, will result in a more nimble force that is able to prevent a repetition of Parakram.[71]

Cold Start is currently in its nascent stages.[72] But the doctrine's continued development and implementation will likely have two major effects. First, it will probably exacerbate regional security-dilemma dynamics. Pakistan has always been a deeply insecure state. Formerly, Pakistanis could expect India's lengthy mobilization schedule to mitigate its military advantages. In the future this may not be the case. As a result, Pakistan will have to maintain a higher state of readiness,[73] and will face incentives to offset Indian strategic advances through increased arms racing and asymmetric warfare. Such behavior could trigger aggressive Indian responses, which would further heighten Pakistani insecurity. These dynamics could undermine recent improvements in Indo-Pakistani relations and increase the probability of crises between the two countries.

Second, Indian doctrinal changes increase the likelihood that Indo-Pakistani crises will escalate rapidly, both within the conventional sphere and from the conventional to the nuclear level. In the conventional realm, Cold Start will enable Indian forces to attack Pakistan quickly, pushing an Indo-Pakistani dispute from the level of political crisis to outright conflict before the Indian government can be deterred from launching an offensive. Vijay Oberoi explains that the decision to attack Pakistan would require "a certain amount of political will. But [Cold Start] makes that political will more likely to be there, since now we can mobilize before world opinion comes down on political leaders and prevents them from acting."[74]

In the nuclear realm, India's Cold Start doctrine would likely force Pakistan to rely more heavily on its strategic deterrent. Brigadier General Khawar Hanif, Pakistan's former defense attaché to the United States, argued that Cold Start will create a "greater justification for Pakistani nuclear weapons" and may increase the danger of nuclear use. "The wider the conventional asymmetry," he maintains, "the lower the nuclear threshold between India and Pakistan. To the extent that India widens the conventional asymmetry through military spending and aggressive doctrinal changes, the nuclear threshold will get lower." Major General Muhammad Mustafa Khan, former director-general (analysis) of Pakistan's Inter-Services Intelligence agency, similarly held that Cold Start "is destabilizing; it is meant to circumvent nuclear deterrence and warning time, . . . [and] it is entirely Pakistan-specific. . . . This will force us to undertake countermeasures," he continues, "and if it becomes too threatening we will have to rely on our nuclear capability."[75] Cold Start thus may erode the firebreak between conventional and nuclear conflict on the subcontinent.

The Indians reportedly anticipate such an outcome at the tactical level and are preparing to fight through Pakistani battlefield nuclear strikes.[76] However, Indian strategists dismiss the possibility of a Pakistani nuclear response against India proper. The Indians maintain that they can carefully calibrate their attack, stopping short of Pakistan's strategic nuclear thresholds and waiting for international diplomatic intervention to end the conflict. As Gurmeet Kanwal explains, "We war-game this all the time and we do not trip their [strategic] red lines." According to Arun Sahgal, Cold Start "will give Pakistan no option but to bring down its nuclear thresholds. But this shouldn't really worry us. We don't think Pakistan will cross the nuclear Rubicon."[77]

However, given the uncertainties that would be inherent in a large-scale Indo-Pakistani conflict, such a benign outcome is hardly guaranteed. For example, an unexpectedly rapid and extensive Indian victory or failure to achieve a quick diplomatic resolution to the conflict could result in a far more extreme Pakistani response than the Indians currently anticipate. India's planning for a carefully controlled limited war with Pakistan could prove to be overly optimistic. As a senior American defense official familiar with Cold Start worries, the Indians "think that they can fight three or four days and the international community will stop it. And they believe that they can fight through a nuclear exchange. But there are unintended consequences. Calibrate a conventional war and nuclear exchange with Pakistan? It doesn't work that way."[78]

It is worth noting that a major Indo-Pakistani crisis could erupt even without a deliberate decision by the Pakistani government to provoke India. The Islamist forces that the Pakistanis have nurtured in recent decades have taken on a life of their own and do not always act at Islamabad's behest. Indeed, they often behave in ways inimical to Pakistani interests, such as launching attacks on Pakistani security forces, government officials, and political figures.[79] And even an improved political and security environment in Kashmir may be insufficient to satisfy the militants; jihad organizations may see eventual control of territory within India proper, rather than the mere liberation of Kashmir, as the true prize in their struggle. Nasr Javed, a Lashkar-e-Toiba official, delivering a speech after the evening prayer at the Quba Mosque in Islamabad on February 5, 2008, stated: "India is also afraid of *jihad*. India fears that if the *Mujahideen* liberated Kashmir through *jihad*, then, it will be very difficult to keep [the] rest of India under control. *Jihad* will spread from Kashmir to other parts of India. The Muslims will be ruling India again." He went on to say, "We want to tell the Kashmiri brothers that the government of Pakistan might have abandoned *jihad* but we have not. Our agenda is clear. We will continue to wage *jihad* and propagate it till eternity. No government can intimidate us. Nobody can stop it—be it the U.S. or Musharraf."[80]

Significantly, the improved security situation in Kashmir may actually facilitate militant violence within India proper and thus increase the likelihood of future Indo-Pakistani conflict. Approximately 140 people died in Islamist terrorist attacks outside of Kashmir in 2007, in locations such as Varanasi, Lucknow, Faizabad, Ajmer, Hyderabad, and Panipat. Meanwhile, 164 civilians were killed in militant attacks in Kashmir during the same year. Kanchan Lakshman argues that even as Pakistan and the militants focus less on fomenting violence within Kahsmir, "J&K is gradually emerging as a launching-pad for terrorist attacks across India. Investigations into these attacks have confirmed that each of them had linkages to the Kashmiri *jihad* in terms of human and logistics support. This shift in the pattern of violence from J&K to other locations offers Pakistan greater 'deniability,' and also enables it to harness the grievances—real or perceived—among the Indian Muslims."[81] Raj Chengappa calls the militants' new approach "a brilliant strategy." By expanding beyond Kashmir and employing local Indian personnel in their operations, the Pakistanis avoid the massive Indian security apparatus in J&K

and ensure that "India can't directly pin responsibility on Pakistan. . . . This enables Pakistan to do what it wants with less opposition and with minimal blame."[82]

Even if this expanding terrorist campaign is not part of a grand Pakistani design, it could have serious consequences for Indo-Pakistani relations. Given Islamabad's tenuous control over the militants, such violence may continue regardless of Pakistani wishes and irrespective of conditions in Kashmir. This would be extremely dangerous. If militants were to stage a large-scale operation similar to the 2001 Parliament attack, the Indians could hold the Pakistani government responsible, regardless of whether Islamabad was actually behind the operation.[83] And with a doctrine that would enable rapid mobilization, India's military response could be far more extensive, and more dangerous, than it was during the 2001–2002 crisis.

By facilitating the outbreak of serious Indo-Pakistani crises in the past, then, nuclear weapons have inspired strategic developments that will make the outbreak and rapid escalation of regional crises more likely in the future. Thus nuclear weapons proliferation not only destabilized South Asia in the first decade since the 1998 tests but is also likely to increase dangers on the subcontinent in the years to come.

CONCLUSION

In this chapter, we discuss nuclear weapons' impact on the current South Asian security environment and speculate as to their likely effects on the region's future. We agree that the Indo-Pakistani security relationship has improved in recent years, but we disagree as to why this occurred. Ganguly argues that recent improvement resulted, to a large degree, from the deterrent effects of nuclear weapons; leaders in both New Delhi and Islamabad realized that in a nuclear environment, continued conflict is prohibitively dangerous; therefore they have decided to pursue peaceful relations. Ganguly expects this pacifying effect to continue in the future. Kapur believes that nuclear weapons have had little to do with current improvements, which he attributes to economic, diplomatic, and nonnuclear strategic factors. And he argues that nuclear weapons, by facilitating past Indo-Pakistani conflict, could destabilize the region in coming years.

ooooo

In chapter 6, we shift our focus away from our competing arguments, instead discussing three issues upon which we agree. First, we argue that our differing approaches to nuclear proliferation actually share important common ground and diverge mainly on which aspect of nuclear-ized crisis behavior one thinks is most important. To a significant degree, the difference between our arguments is one of emphasis on either the stable outcomes of past South Asian militarized disputes or the danger-ous processes by which these disputes erupted and escalated. Second, we maintain that the possible deployment of missile defense in South Asia, far from stabilizing the subcontinent, is likely to create incentives for aggressive regional behavior. And finally, we argue that nuclear weapons are unlikely to resolve the central security threat currently facing South Asia: Islamist militants not fully under the control of any government. Instead of relying on nuclear deterrence, India and Pakistan should thor-oughly rethink their approaches to national security, adopting policies far outside their traditional comfort zones.

6 | Three Points of Agreement

This book focuses primarily on our disagreements about nuclear weapons proliferation in South Asia. First, we develop competing theoretical accounts of proliferation's strategic effects. Ganguly argues that nuclear weapons, because of their inherent destructive properties, induce even the most intransigent adversaries to exercise restraint and prevent the escalation of violent conflicts. Kapur's strategic pessimism maintains that nuclear weapons, by providing a shield against all-out retaliation and attracting international attention, can increase the incentive for weak, dissatisfied powers to engage in destabilizing behavior. Second, we show how our theoretical approaches explain past Indo-Pakistani strategic behavior. Ganguly argues that the nuclearization of the subcontinent actually reduced the possibilities of full-scale war between the two long-standing adversaries. Cognizant of the dangers of nuclear escalation, both sides chose to exercise restraint and pursue a peace process. According to Kapur, nuclear weapons contributed to rising regional tensions during the proliferation process, facilitating the outbreak of significant Indo-Pakistani militarized crises and playing only a limited role in their resolution. Finally, we examine the current South Asian security environment and offer predictions regarding the future. Ganguly argues that reductions in Indo-Pakistani tensions stemmed in large part from India's willingness to resort to a strategy of coercive diplomacy in the aftermath of the Pakistan-based terrorist attacks in December 2001. India adopted this strategy largely because embarking on a conventional war against Pakistan invited the possibility of nuclear escalation. He also maintains that nuclear deterrence is likely to ensure regional stability in the future. Kapur claims that recent improvements in Indo-Pakistani relations have resulted from nonnuclear strategic, domestic, and diplomatic factors. And he predicts that nuclear weapons' past effects on the regional security environment will destabilize South Asia in years to come.

In this chapter we shift our focus away from our disagreements to discuss three nuclear-related issues upon which we agree. First, we revisit the theoretical bases of our arguments and ask how far apart they actually are. We suggest that in truth our arguments share a number of important similarities and that the difference between our approaches is largely one of emphasis. Our assessments of nuclear weapons' effects on South Asia differ because we disagree as to which aspects of regional crisis behavior are most important; Ganguly believes that the relatively benign outcomes of Indo-Pakistani crises matter most, while Kapur focuses on the dangerous process of crisis outbreak and escalation.

Second, we discuss the impact that the possible Indian acquisition of ballistic missile defense capabilities would have on strategic stability in the region. We contend that such a course would likely prove to be destabilizing, increasing the incentives for arms racing and possibly for the first use of nuclear weapons.

Third, we examine the November 2008 terrorist attacks on Mumbai and discuss their implications for the future of Indo-Pakistani relations and regional security in South Asia. We argue that the Mumbai attacks point up the fundamental security problem facing South Asia in the future: Nonstate actors, whom Pakistan employed over past decades as asymmetric weapons against India, have taken on a life of their own. They now behave in ways that are not only damaging to India but also detrimental to Pakistan's national interests. Unfortunately, neither India nor Pakistan currently possesses the conventional military, intelligence, or policing capabilities needed to rein them in. And nuclear weapons, which facilitated Pakistan's original adoption of an asymmetric warfare strategy, are useless in combating militants; prevent large-scale Indian retaliation against Pakistan, which could make Islamabad's continued tolerance of anti-Indian militancy prohibitively costly; and pose security risks of their own. Devising a solution to this dilemma will constitute the region's main security challenge in coming years.

OPTIMISM VS. PESSIMISM AS OUTCOME VS. PROCESS

In this book, we offer divergent theoretical views as to nuclear weapons' effects on the South Asian security environment. How far apart are our competing positions? Do we share any common ground? We maintain that, despite our differences, our arguments are not wholly at odds with each other. While nuclear optimist and pessimist positions are sometimes seen as opposites, the differences between the two camps may be exaggerated. Both of us agree that nuclear weapons proliferation will not lead to the deliberate outbreak of large-scale war in South Asia. Neither Indian nor Pakistani leaders wish to initiate a conflict that could end in catastrophic losses or, potentially, national annihilation. We differ, however, on the importance that we assign to the possibility that catastrophic conflict could occur even though neither the Indians nor the Pakistanis intend it. Ganguly, and optimists generally, recognize that large-scale conflict, including nuclear escalation, could eventually occur in a nuclear environment; they do not claim that such an outcome is impossible. They focus, however, on the relatively benign nature of past history. Despite strained relations and numerous crises, India and Pakistan have consistently managed to avoid large-scale war or nuclear confrontation, thanks in large part to nuclear weapons' pacifying effects. In Ganguly's view, the future is likely to resemble the past, with nuclear deterrence preventing catastrophe, even in the face of continued tensions and disputes. Thus disaster in a nuclear South Asia remains highly unlikely.

Kapur, and pessimists generally, acknowledge that disaster has not occurred in a nuclear South Asia; they recognize that India and Pakistan have managed to avoid large-scale conflict and catastrophic escalation despite heightened regional tensions and continued crises. These scholars, however, emphasize the considerable dangers inherent in repeated Indo-Pakistani confrontations. Despite past crises' relatively benign outcomes, India and Pakistan have only narrowly avoided large-scale conventional and potentially even nuclear conflict. Moreover, nuclear deterrence was not primarily responsible for these fortunate results. In Kapur's view, then, the region's future may not resemble the past. India and Pakistan may not be able to defuse their next confrontation before reaching the point of major conventional or nuclear conflict. Thus disaster remains a real possibility in a nuclear South Asia.

Is Ganguly's view correct? Or does Kapur's approach prevail? The answer to this question depends on the importance that one assigns to the outcomes of South Asian militarized disputes versus the processes by which those disputes erupted, escalated, and were resolved. Does one care more about what actually happened in past Indo-Pakistani confrontations or what could have happened? Those who take an outcome-based approach will tend to be optimistic about nuclear weapons' regional effects. For in the end, confrontations and crises in a nuclear South Asia have always been resolved without large-scale escalation. Those who take a process-based approach will tend to be pessimistic about nuclear weapons' regional effects. For despite generally benign results in the past, repeatedly navigating through the outbreak, escalation, and resolution of Indo-Pakistani crises is an uncertain and risky endeavor.

Whether an outcome- or a process-based approach is superior, then, is a matter of judgment. Deductive reasoning cannot determine whether benign past outcomes are more important than future risky processes or vice versa. This does not mean, of course, that serious differences between the two approaches do not remain. In the end, Ganguly's focus on outcome leads to the conclusion that nuclear weapons have made South Asia substantially safer, while Kapur's focus on process leads to the conclusion that the region is significantly more dangerous. And these differences affect not only our analysis of past cases of nuclear proliferation but also our view of potential proliferation in the future. If the outcomes of future crises between nuclear powers are likely to resemble those of the past, then the possibility of further proliferation elsewhere around the globe is not particularly worrisome. Indeed, it may even be desirable. But if the processes of crisis outbreak, escalation, and resolution in a nuclear environment are dangerous and uncertain, the results of future disputes may not resemble those of the past. If this is the case, the possibility of future proliferation is extremely worrisome. Thus we agree that it is possible to overstate the nature of our theoretical disagreement, which can be reduced to a difference in the importance that we assign to crisis outcome versus process. Nonetheless, that difference remains important and leads us to very different views of proliferation's effects in South Asia and its likely implications for future nuclear powers.

Below, we shift our discussion to another pressing South Asian nuclear issue: missile defense.

MISSILE DEFENSE IN SOUTH ASIA: A DANGEROUS PROPOSITION

Despite its strong historical opposition to ballistic missile defense, the Indian government has recently become interested in acquiring missile defense capabilities. This interest can be traced to the Bush administration's decision to abandon the U.S. commitment to the 1972 Anti-Ballistic Missile Treaty. In a remarkable shift, India became one of the first states cautiously to embrace the administration's policy.[1] Since then India has undertaken small but significant steps toward the acquisition of a BMD capability, exploring possible acquisition of Israeli, Russian, and most recently American missile defense technology.[2] It has also engaged in domestic efforts to develop BMD, apparently meeting with some degree of success.[3] Indian officials have been vocal in their advocacy of missile defense. According to Indian president A. P. J. Kalam, "In the next two decades, anti-ballistic missile defense systems are going to be a major force ... to guard against nuclear weapons attack."[4] India's chief military scientist, V. K. Saraswat of the Defence Research and Development Organisation, argues that "if I keep quiet and wait for [a missile] to fall on my city ... a lot of damage is done. It is essential you have a system which will first take on that kind of threat."[5] Despite the efforts under way, India is not yet close to acquiring and deploying a viable ballistic missile defense program.[6]

Some analysts have written sympathetically of India's new interest in missile defense. Ashley Tellis, for example, identifies a threefold rationale for an Indian BMD capability, focusing on the insecurity of Pakistan's nuclear arsenal, Pakistan's ongoing attempts to coerce India by prosecuting a strategy of low-intensity conflict from behind the shield of nuclear deterrence, and the dangers of Pakistani horizontal nuclear proliferation, as exemplified by the activities of the A. Q. Khan network.[7] Rajesh Basrur goes further, maintaining that Indian leaders are *obligated* to pursue missile defense capabilities, since "it is incumbent upon the government to take at least some steps to protect its citizens against the small risk of deterrence failure by error, accident, or design."[8]

Such arguments are not without merit, particularly given concerns regarding the security of Pakistan's nuclear arsenal and the concomitant dangers of unauthorized Pakistani nuclear use. Nonetheless, we believe that, on balance, Indian missile defense would be strategically undesirable, even if it were technologically feasible and financially viable. The danger of missile defense, in our view, is essentially the same as that of counterforce nuclear capabilities.[9] During the Cold War, the United States and the Soviet Union developed nuclear weapons sufficiently accurate and powerful to destroy each other's nuclear forces, even when those forces were located in hardened silos. The main purpose of such "counterforce" weapons was to limit damage to the attacking state in the event of a nuclear conflict. If the attacker's counterforce could destroy a significant portion of its adversary's weapons while those weapons were still on the ground, the adversary's ability to harm the attacker would be proportionately reduced.[10]

Although this might appear to be an attractive outcome, counterforce actually had dangerous implications, threatening to create incentives for both sides to use nuclear weapons first in the event of a crisis. If the leaders of a state believed that striking their adversary first with counterforce could significantly limit the adversary's ability to harm them, they might be tempted to do so. And if the leaders of the adversary state anticipated being struck with counterforce, they might decide to launch their own weapons first, to prevent them from being destroyed on the ground. Counterforce also created incentives for both sides to arms race. The larger a state's nuclear arsenal, the more difficulty its adversary would have in attempting to destroy that arsenal through a counterforce strike. Opponents in a counterforce environment might seek to obtain additional warheads, thereby setting off a spiral of weapons acquisitions.[11]

Unlike counterforce weapons, missile defense capabilities would destroy the enemy's nuclear forces after launch, rather than on the ground. This technical difference aside, however, BMD would achieve much the same strategic result as counterforce weapons, preventing a state from effectively using its nuclear forces to retaliate against its adversary. As with counterforce weapons, this could create first-strike incentives. If a state feared that its adversary was contemplating an attack against its nuclear forces or command and control, and its adversary also possessed a missile defense capability, the state could be sorely tempted to launch its forces first. This would get the state's forces off the ground before they were hit by the expected attack and would maximize the number of weapons the adversary's BMD would have to intercept simultaneously, thereby increasing the likelihood that some of the weapons would get through the system and reach enemy soil. If the state did not strike first, and a significant percentage of its nuclear forces were destroyed or incapacitated in the enemy's initial attack, the enemy's BMD might be able to absorb the state's remaining forces. In this situation, the state would be unable to use its nuclear forces to retaliate against an attack and would thus be rendered essentially defenseless.[12]

In addition to possible first-strike temptations, a state facing a BMD-equipped adversary might have strong incentives to arms race. The more weapons the state can launch at the enemy, the greater the likelihood that it could exceed the missile defense system's capabilities, which would ensure that at least some of its weapons reach enemy territory. Thus the state could seek to expand the size of its nuclear arsenal.[13]

These strategic effects could adversely impact India's security relationships with its two principal adversaries, Pakistan and China. Pakistan possesses a relatively small nuclear arsenal, probably numbering about sixty warheads.[14] Even a modest Indian missile defense capability could erode Pakistan's ability to retaliate after an Indian attack on its nuclear weapons or command and control. This scenario would be especially threatening when combined with India's growing air defense capabilities, which will be able to shoot down Pakistani bombers with increasing effectiveness.[15] An Indian first strike on Pakistan would be extremely dangerous; even a few surviving Pakistani nuclear weapons could inflict untold damage on India's civilian and military infrastructure. Unfortunately, such a scenario is not impossible. A risk-prone Indian decision maker in the midst of a crisis might be tempted to launch first, gambling that Indian conventional and nuclear advantages, combined with missile defense, could limit Indian damage to acceptable levels while destroying Pakistan as a viable entity.

Given the violence of the two countries' past relationship, Pakistani leaders are likely to seriously consider such a possibility and respond accordingly. This would almost certainly entail augmenting Pakistan's nuclear arsenal. As Pakistani defense analyst Ayesha Siddiqa argues, in the event that India acquires BMD capability, Pakistan will "seek to increase the number of missiles to make sure it has enough to evade the [Indian] shield."[16] In addition, Pakistani leaders could escalate to the strategic level more quickly in a crisis, fearing that they might lose their nuclear weapons to an Indian first-strike and BMD capability if they do not use them quickly. As Dinshaw Mistry argues, "As long as the India-Pakistan region is crisis prone, . . . [missile defense] will be destabilizing because it undermines crisis stability."[17]

An Indian BMD system's effects on China might be similar, though probably significantly less severe given the size of China's nuclear arsenal. The Chinese possess approximately 240 nuclear warheads.[18] Thus an Indian missile defense capability, particularly if it was limited in scope, would be considerably less threatening to the Chinese than it would be to the Pakistanis. Still, India's ability to reduce the efficacy of a Chinese second-strike capability could lead the Chinese to increase the size of their nuclear arsenal and could also make them more likely to strike first in the event of a crisis.[19] China could also respond to Indian BMD by renewing its nuclear and ballistic missile transfers to Pakistan, in an effort to offset Indian capabilities and bolster Beijing's long-standing ally.[20] Such negative reactions are particularly likely given India and China's checkered history,[21] and past Sino-Indian tension over Indian nuclear capabilities.[22]

Missile defense, then, could have significantly destabilizing effects in South Asia, creating incentives for costly arms races and possibly increasing the likelihood that states will be tempted to strike first with nuclear weapons during a crisis. Thus, despite BMD's appeal to Indian political leaders and some regional analysts, we believe that India should forgo a missile defense capability. It would do better to concentrate on increasing the security and viability of its own arsenal, rather than taking steps that could potentially threaten the nuclear forces of its adversaries.

Below, we raise a final issue: the state of the South Asian security environment in the wake of the November 2008 Mumbai terror attacks.

SOUTH ASIA'S SORCERER'S APPRENTICE PROBLEM

On November 26, 2008, a group of ten terrorists attacked the city of Mumbai. Over the next three days, they went on a killing spree at a Jewish cultural center known as the Nariman House, the Oberoi-Trident and Taj Mahal hotels, the nearby Leopold Café, the Chhatrapati Shivaji railway terminus, and the Bhikaji Cama Children's Hospital.[23] By the time Indian police and paramilitary forces finally overpowered them, the terrorists had killed more than 160 people and wounded hundreds more.[24] Indian authorities ascertained that the terrorists were members of a long-banned but nonetheless active Pakistan-based terrorist organization, the Lashkar-e-Toiba.[25] Western governments subsequently supported New Delhi's conclusions, and the United Nations levied sanctions against LeT's parent organization, Jamaat-ud-Dawa, declaring it a terrorist entity.[26] The Mumbai assault became the latest in a series of attacks on Indian cities conducted by terror groups operating within Pakistan.[27]

Following these events, a single question reverberated from New Delhi to Washington: Were the Mumbai attacks not simply the work of Pakistan-based militants but actually orchestrated by the Pakistani government? In an important sense, this was the wrong question to ask. During the 1980s and the 1990s, the Pakistani government nurtured terror organizations such as Lashkar-e-Toiba as tools of asymmetric warfare against the Soviet occupation of Afghanistan and then against Indian rule in Jammu and Kashmir. The jihadis were armed and trained by elements of the Pakistani military and intelligence services, and funded by a sophisticated international financial network. In addition, they have enjoyed street-level popularity and remained a useful means of combating India's presence in Kashmir. Consequently, the Pakistani government balked at opportunities to shut them down completely.[28]

Now, however, the Pakistanis' strategy has given rise to what we call South Asia's "sorcerer's apprentice" problem. The jihadi organizations, like the magic brooms in Goethe's tale, have taken on a life of their own; along with the government, the army, and the intelligence services, such groups now comprise one of the main centers of gravity within Pakistan. As a result, the militants are in a position to establish and follow through on their own policy. Like Goethe's brooms, they often act against the interests of their creators, attacking security personnel, assassinating government officials, and seizing large swaths of territory within Pakistan, as well as launching attacks on India that could trigger a regional conflagration.[29] The relevant question, then, is not whether the Pakistani government was directly responsible for the Mumbai attacks. Rather, it is who will now play the role of sorcerer and rein in the jihadis.

The natural candidates for this role would be either the Pakistani or the Indian government. But the Mumbai attacks have made painfully clear that neither side is currently up to the task. The Pakistani government has solemnly pledged not to allow its soil to be used as a launching ground for anti-Indian terrorism.[30] But the Mumbai assault demonstrates that Pakistan is unable to make good on this promise. The Indians, for their part, are unable to anticipate or repel such attacks. Although the Indian government had received credible warnings of a seaborne terrorist operation, the Mumbai attackers caught the Indians completely unawares. And once the assault began, Indian security personnel took nearly three days to rout just a handful of attackers.[31]

India does enjoy conventional military superiority over Pakistan. This advantage does, not, however, afford the Indians many options for playing the role of regional sorcerer. Their most plausible strategy would be to strike across the line of control against suspected terrorist camps in Pakistani Kashmir.[32] But such attacks, even if successful, would yield only limited benefits because Kashmiri militant camps are transitory in nature and lack high-value human and physical infrastructure.[33]

Because strikes on terrorist camps are not likely to be effective, the Indians might threaten to launch large-scale attacks against Pakistan proper if the Pakistanis fail to prevent further terrorism against India. Although India would eventually prevail, victory in the ensuing conflict would be costly.[34] Nonetheless, such a large-scale confrontation could render continued tolerance for anti-Indian militancy prohibitively expensive for Pakistan, thus finally convincing the Pakistanis to fully renounce the jihadi option. Even if Indian leaders decided that the potential benefits of such a policy were worth the costs, however, it would remain infeasible. The reason is simple: Pakistan's nuclear capacity. Given the danger of nuclear escalation, it would be too risky for the Indians to launch attacks deep into Pakistani territory. In the past, India has been willing to contemplate limited conflict with a nuclear-armed Pakistan. But Pakistan's nuclear capacity has prompted the Indians explicitly to eschew the possibility of launching a full-scale attack on the Pakistanis.[35] This is unlikely to change in the near future.[36]

Neither India's nor Pakistan's intelligence, police, or conventional military forces are able to solve South Asia's sorcerer's apprentice problem. And the countries' nuclear capabilities are largely useless as well. Islamabad's nuclear capacity facilitated its initial adoption of a low-intensity conflict strategy against India during the 1980s and 1990s, preventing large-scale Indian retaliation while Pakistan-backed militants launched attacks in Indian Kashmir. Nuclear weapons cannot now be used to target the militants who flourished as a result of this strategy and currently wreak havoc in both India and Pakistan. Nuclear weapons also limit India's future military options against Pakistan, preventing New Delhi from taking action that, however costly, might convince the Pakistanis to revisit their tolerance for anti-Indian militancy.

Finally, nuclear weapons pose a danger in the context of Pakistan's unstable domestic political and security environment. Pakistan's nuclear arsenal is under tight control of the army, the most powerful institution in the country. The army has enormous incentives to ensure the weapons' security, and there is no evidence to suggest that they face any immediate threat. Still, in an extreme situation, the Pakistani arsenal might be vulnerable. For example, if Pakistan attempts to move weapons during a crisis with India, militants might be able to seize them as they are being transported—particularly if the jihadis have the assistance of insiders with access to the weapons' transport schedule. Of course, even if they managed to steal a weapon, the militants would still have to maintain possession of it and determine how to use it. These would be difficult tasks. Nonetheless, Pakistani nuclear security is a genuine concern. Nuclear weapons thus are unhelpful in addressing the challenge of Islamist militancy in South Asia; they might even potentially pose dangers of their own.[37]

What, then, is the solution to South Asia's sorcerer's apprentice problem? The situation will require a radical rethinking of the region's security framework. Both India and Pakistan must adopt policies that transcend their traditional comfort zones. The Pakistani government must truly forswear militancy, ending support for the jihadis and accepting international military and financial assistance in crushing them. The Pakistanis need to recognize that the costs of supporting militancy outweigh its benefits and that Mumbai may present it with a final opportunity to get control of the situation. If the government does not act against the militants soon, it may lose control of the state or find itself drawn into a catastrophic conflict with India in the wake of another terrorist attack.

Islamabad's initial response to allegations of a Pakistani link to the Mumbai attacks was one of denial and defiance. However, given mounting evidence of a Pakistani connection to the attacks, as well as American, British, and UN pressure, Pakistan changed its position, arresting militant leaders and shutting down Jamaat-ud-Dawa.[38] In the past, such Pakistani actions have been mostly cosmetic; in the wake of government crackdowns, terror organizations have changed their names and quickly resumed their activities.[39] Therefore, it remains to be seen whether Islamabad's current policy will have any lasting impact. Given the track record of past Pakistani governments, it seems doubtful that the fledgling democratic regime of President Asif Ali Zardari will have the ability or interest needed to move seriously against the militants. But only time will tell.

The Indians, for their part, must start to take their own security more seriously. In 1991, after suffering a major financial crisis, the Indian government came to terms with the failures of its socialist development model and adopted a new, free-market approach to economic growth. India must use the Mumbai crisis to wholly revamp its security infrastructure. The Indians appear to have begun this process. Soon after the attacks the government announced that it was enhancing its maritime security capabilities, creating an FBI-like National Investigative Agency, increasing intelligence sharing, improving the training and equipment of police and domestic security forces, and strengthening antiterrorism laws.[40] The Indians must follow through on these initiatives. In addition, they must address the legitimate concerns of their own Muslim community, including the long-aggrieved Kashmiri population, so that overseas terrorists do not find willing collaborators within India. If they fail to take these steps, the country's impressive military and economic gains of recent years will be for naught. Sophisticated conventional military capabilities, and even a nuclear arsenal, mean little when ordinary citizens are not safe from the threat of gunmen in the railway stations, streets, hospitals, and hotels of their own cities. And in the absence of major security improvements, international corporations will lose interest in India, viewing the country as excessively dangerous and refusing to do business there.

None of the steps outlined above will provide an overnight solution to the problems laid bare by the Mumbai attacks. But, in time, they can help South Asia create its own modern-day sorcerer, dealing with the militant forces that Pakistan has unleashed over recent decades without triggering a large-scale war or nuclear conflagration. If the region fails to meet this challenge, its most pressing security challenge will go unaddressed. And, as a result, South Asia's story, unlike Goethe's, will not have a happy ending.

Notes

1. INTRODUCTION

1. See, for example, Kenneth N. Waltz, "For Better: Nuclear Weapons Preserve an Imperfect Peace," in *The Spread of Nuclear Weapons: A Debate Renewed*, Scott D. Sagan and Kenneth N. Waltz (New York: Norton, 2003), 117; K. Subrahmanyam, "India and the International Nuclear Order," in *Nuclear India in the Twenty-first Century*, ed. D. R. SarDesai and Raju G. C. Thomas (New York: Palgrave Macmillan, 2002), 83; John J. Mearsheimer, "Here We Go Again," *New York Times*, May 17, 1998; Scott D. Sagan, "For Worse: Till Death Do Us Part," in *The Spread of Nuclear Weapons*, Sagan and Waltz, 106–7; P. R. Chari, "Nuclear Restraint, Nuclear Risk Reduction, and the Security-Insecurity Paradox in South Asia," in *The Stability-Instability Paradox: Nuclear Weapons and Brinksmanship in South Asia*, ed. Michael Krepon and Chris Gagné (Washington, D.C.: Stimson Center, 2001), 16; Kanti Bajpai, "The Fallacy of an Indian Deterrent," in *India's Nuclear Deterrent: Pokhran II and Beyond*, ed. Amitabh Mattoo (New Delhi: HarAnand, 1999).

2. S. Paul Kapur and Šumit Ganguly, "The Transformation of U.S.-India Relations: An Explanation for the Rapprochement and Prospects for the Future," *Asian Survey* 47, no. 4 (July–August 2007): 645, 648–49.

3. See CIA, *World Factbook*, https://www.cia.gov/library/publications/the-world-factbook/geos/pk.html.

4. From 2001 to 2006 the Indian defense budget increased by 60 percent, from $13.81 billion to $22.1 billion. Between 2007 and 2012 India is predicted to

spend up to $40 billion on weapons procurement, including fighter aircraft, artillery, submarines, and armor. See Jane's World Defense Industry, "JWDI Briefing: India's Defence Industry," September 18, 2007; Heather Timmons and Somini Sengupta, "Building a Modern Arsenal in India," *New York Times*, August 31, 2007. See also Rodney W. Jones, "Conventional Military and Strategic Stability in South Asia," South Asian Strategic Stability Unit Research Paper No. 1, March 2005.

5. See Foster Klug, "Senate Gives Final OK to U.S.-India Nuclear Deal," Associated Press, October 2, 2008.

6. See Nahal Toosi, "Pakistan Likely to Stay on Course on War on Terror," Associated Press, August 19, 2008.

7. One important exception is Devin T. Hagerty, *The Consequences of Nuclear Proliferation: Lessons from South Asia* (Cambridge: MIT Press, 1997). For two early critiques of the inordinate reliance on deductive logic in the development of deterrence theory, see Philip Green, *Deadly Logic: The Theory of Nuclear Deterrence* (Columbus: Ohio State University Press, 1966), and Alexander L. George and Richard Smoke, *Deterrence in American Foreign Policy: Theory and Practice* (New York: Columbia University Press, 1974).

8. The classic statement remains Kenneth N. Waltz, *The Spread of Nuclear Weapons: More May Be Better* Adelphi Paper 171 (London: International Institute of Strategic Studies, 1981).

9. Jordan Seng, "Less Is More: Command and Control Advantages of Minor Nuclear States," *Security Studies* 6, no. 4 (Summer 1997): 50–92.

10. David J. Karl, "Proliferation Pessimism and Emerging Nuclear Powers," *International Security* 21, no. 3 (Winter 1996–1997): 87–119.

2. THE HISTORY OF INDO-PAKISTANI CONFLICT

1. Radha Kumar, "The Troubled History of Partition," *Foreign Affairs* 76, no. 1 (January–February 1997).

2. Sir Penderel Moon, *Divide and Quit* (Berkeley: University of California Press, 1962).

3. Sisir Gupta, *Kashmir: A Study in India-Pakistan Relations* (Bombay: Asia Publishing House, 1967).

4. Šumit Ganguly, *Conflict Unending: India-Pakistan Tensions since 1947* (New York: Columbia University Press, and New Delhi: Oxford University Press, 2001).

5. Praveen Swami, *India, Pakistan, and the Secret Jihad: The Covert War in Kashmir, 1947–2004* (London; Routledge, 2006).

6. Francis Robinson, *Separatism among Indian Muslims: The Politics of the United Provinces, 1860–1923* (Cambridge: Cambridge University Press, 1974).

7. The literature on the partition of the subcontinent is vast. See, for example, C. H. Phillips and Mary Doreen Wainwright, eds., *The Partition of India: Policies and Perspectives, 1935–1947* (London: Allen and Unwin, 1970); Anita Inder Singh, *The Origins of the Partition of India* (New York: Oxford University Press, 1970); Mushirul Hasan, *India's Partition: Process, Strategy, and Mobilization* (Delhi: Oxford University Press, 1990); and Yasmin Khan, *The Great Partition: The Making of India and Pakistan* (New Haven: Yale University Press, 2007).

8. Ian Copland, *The Princes of India in the Endgame of Empire, 1917–1947* (Cambridge: Cambridge University Press, 2002). See also Ramachandra Guha, *India after Gandhi: The History of the World's Largest Democracy* (New Delhi: Macmillan, 2007).

9. V. P. Menon, *The Story of the Integration of the Indian States* (New York: Macmillan, 1956).

10. The question of Kashmir's borders at the time of partition is controversial. For a discussion of the controversy and an assessment of the evidence, see Shereen Ilahi, "The Radcliffe Boundary Commission and the Fate of Kashmir," *India Review* 2, no. 1 (January 2003): 77–102.

11. Jyoti Bhusan Das Gupta, *Jammu and Kashmir* (The Hague: Martinus Nijhoff, 1968).

12. The details pertaining to Pakistan's involvement in the conflict can be found in Akbar Khan, *Raiders in Kashmir* (Karachi: Pak Publishers, 1970). See also H. V. Hodson, *The Great Divide: Britain, India, Pakistan* (New York: Oxford University Press, 1997).

13. For details see Andrew Whitehead, *A Mission in Kashmir* (London: Penguin Global, 2008).

14. Sumit Ganguly, *The Crisis in Kashmir: Portents of War, Hopes of Peace* (Cambridge and Washington, D.C.: Cambridge University Press and the Woodrow Wilson Center Press, 1997) 10–11.

15. On the dispatch of Indian troops, see Lionel Protip Sen, *Slender Was the Thread: Kashmir Confrontation, 1947–48* (New Delhi: Orient Longman, 1969).

16. Note that precisely who made the decision to send Indian troops to Kashmir and at what juncture remains the subject of scholarly dispute. Accord-

ing to Alastair Lamb, Indian troops entered Kashmir *before* Maharaja Hari Singh had signed the Instrument of Accession. Lamb also alleges that the Instrument of Accession may not have been signed at all. Prem Shankar Jha seeks to refute these allegations through a close examination of British colonial archives and through interviews with key individuals who were present at the time of the accession. Chandrasekhar Dasgupta maintains that senior British military officers serving the Indian government, as well as Lord Louis Mountbatten, were loath to deploy the Indian Army in Kashmir after the tribal invasion. Their acquiescence came about only after Prime Minister Nehru and Home Affairs Minister Sardar Vallabhai Patel insisted that Kashmir's defense was critical to India's national security. Finally, Alex Von Tunzelmann maintains that Sardar Vallabhai Patel made the decision to send Indian troops to Kashmir to ensure its accession to India. See Alastair Lamb, *Kashmir: A Disputed Legacy, 1846–1990* (Karachi: Oxford University Press, 1991); Lamb, *The Birth of a Tragedy: Kashmir, 1947* (Hertingfordbury: Roxford Books, 1994); Prem Shankar Jha, *Kashmir, 1947: Rival Versions of History* (New Delhi: Oxford University Press, 1996); Chandrasekhar Dasgupta, *War and Diplomacy in Kashmir, 1947–48* (New Delhi: Sage Publications, 2002); Alex Von Tunzelmann, *Indian Summer: The Secret History of the End of an Empire* (New York: Henry Holt, 2007).

17. Sen, *Slender Was the Thread*, 159–61.

18. Ganguly, *Conflict Unending*.

19. Raju G. C. Thomas, *Indian Defense Policy* (Princeton: Princeton University Press, 1986).

20. Dasgupta, *War and Diplomacy*.

21. See Šumit Ganguly, "Deterrence Failure Revisited: The Indo-Pakistani War of 1965," *Journal of Strategic Studies* 13, no. 4 (December 1990): 77–93, and Ganguly, *Conflict Unending*.

22. Russell Brines, *The Indo-Pakistani Conflict* (New York: Pall Mall, 1968).

23. Robert Jackson, *South Asian Crisis: India, Pakistan, and Bangla Desh* (New York: Praeger, 1975).

24. See Sisson and Rose, *War and Secession*.

25. See Ganguly, *Conflict Unending*.

26. See the *Hamoodur Rehman Commission of Inquiry into the 1971 War, Report as Declassified by the Government of Pakistan*, pt. 4, "Military Aspect" (Lahore, Pakistan: Vanguard Books, 2000); Amin, *Pakistan's Foreign Policy*, 43, 72; Ganguly, *Conflict Unending*, 71–72; S. M. Burke and Lawrence Ziring, *Pakistan's Foreign Policy: An Historical Analysis* (Karachi: Oxford University

Press, 1990), 420–21.

27. See text of Simla Agreement, 204–6; Chari, "The Simla Agreement: An Indian Appraisal," 61; and Pervaiz Iqbal Cheema, "The Simla Agreement: Current Relevance?" 135, all in P. R. Chari and Pervaiz Iqbal Cheema, *The Simla Agreement, 1972: Its Wasted Promise* (New Delhi: Manohar, 2001).

28. See S. Paul Kapur, *Dangerous Deterrent: Nuclear Weapons Proliferation and Conflict in South Asia* (Stanford, Calif.: Stanford University Press, 2007), 64–66.

29. The All Jammu and Kashmir National Conference was Kashmir's leading political party.

30. Šumit Ganguly, "Explaining the Kashmir Insurgency: Political Mobilization and Institutional Decay," *International Security* 21, no. 2 (1996): 80, 84–85, 99; V. P. Malik, *Kargil: From Surprise to Victory* (New Delhi: HarperCollins, 2006), 143–45, 147, 158–60, 164, 167–68, 170, 283; Ganguly, *The Crisis in Kashmir*, 65–73; Wirsing, *India, Pakistan, and the Kashmir Dispute*, 113–18; Schofield, *Kashmir in Conflict*, 137–38; Sumantra Bose, *Kashmir: Roots of Conflict, Paths to Peace* (Cambridge, Mass.: Harvard University Press, 2003), 51, 97–101, 107–35.

31. Wirsing, *India, Pakistan, and the Kashmir Dispute*, 121, 134; John Lancaster and Kamran Khan, "Extremist Groups Renew Activity in Pakistan; Support of Kashmir Militants Is at Odds with War on Terrorism," *Washington Post*, February 8, 2003; Malik, *Kashmir*, 295–98; Sheikh Mushtaq, "Kashmir Violence Dips to All-Time Low," Reuters, April 1, 2007; and www.prio.no/CSCW/Datasets/Armed-Conflict/Battle-Deaths/The-Battle-Deaths-Dataset-version-30/.

32. For the full text of the NPT, see www.iaea.org/Publications/Documents/Infcircs/Others/infcirc140.pdf. The NPT is the foundation of a broader nonproliferation regime consisting of bilateral and multilateral agreements designed to prevent proliferation by monitoring and limiting the transfer of nuclear materials and technology and by preventing nuclear testing.

33. See Mitchell Reiss, *Bridled Ambition: Why Countries Constrain Their Nuclear Capabilities* (Washington, D.C.: Woodrow Wilson Center Press, 1995), 45–88.

34. See Reiss, *Bridled Ambition*; William C. Potter, "The Politics of Denuclearization: The Cases of Belarus, Kazakhstan, and Ukraine," Occasional Paper No. 22, Henry L. Stimson Center, Washington, D.C., April 1995.

35. See Šumit Ganguly, "India's Pathway to Pokhran II: The Prospects and Sources of New Delhi's Nuclear Weapons Program," *International Security* 23, no. 4 (1999): 148–77.

36. See Samina Ahmed, "Pakistan's Nuclear Weapons Program: Turning Points and Nuclear Choices," *International Security* 32, no. 4 (1999): 178–204.

37. Jaswant Singh, "Against Nuclear Apartheid," *Foreign Affairs* 77, no. 5 (September–October 1998).

38. See Hagerty, *The Consequences of Nuclear Proliferation*, 124, 131–32; Kapur, *Dangerous Deterrent*.

39. Leonard Spector, *The Undeclared Bomb* (Cambridge, Mass.: Ballinger Publishing, 1988), 70.

40. Devin Hagerty, *The Consequences of Nuclear Proliferation: Lessons from South Asia* (Cambridge, Mass.: MIT Press, 1998), 188.

41. Kenneth Waltz, "The Spread of Nuclear Weapons: More May Be Better," Adelphi Papers 171 (London: International Institute of Strategic Studies, 1981).

42. Sagan and Waltz, *The Spread of Nuclear Weapons*, 106–7. See also P. R. Chari, "Nuclear Restraint, Nuclear Risk Reduction, and the Security-Insecurity Paradox in South Asia," in *The Stability-Instability Paradox: Nuclear Weapons and Brinksmanship in South Asia*, ed. Michael Krepon and Chris Gagné (Washington, D.C.: Stimson Center, 2001), 16. See also Kanti Bajpai, "The Fallacy of an Indian Deterrent," in *India's Nuclear Deterrent: Pokhran II and Beyond*, ed. Amitabh Mattoo (New Delhi: HarAnand, 1999); Samina Ahmed, "Security Dilemmas of Nuclear-Armed Pakistan," *Third World Quarterly* 21, no. 5 (2001): 781–93.

43. Waltz, "For Better," in *The Spread of Nuclear Weapons*, Sagan and Waltz, 117.

44. Sagan, "For the Worse," in *The Spread of Nuclear Weapons*, Sagan and Waltz, 91–92.

3. COMPETING ARGUMENTS
ABOUT SOUTH ASIAN PROLIFERATION

1. Scott D. Sagan, "The Perils of Proliferation in South Asia," *Asian Survey* 41, no. 6 (November–December 2001): 1064–86.

2. Stephen M. Walt, *Revolution and War* (Ithaca: Cornell University Press, 1997).

3. John W. Lewis and Xue Litai, *China Builds the Bomb* (Palo Alto: Stanford University Press, 1988).

4. Lyle Goldstein, "Return to Zhenbao Island: Who Started Shooting and Why It Matters," *China Quarterly* 168 (December 2001): 985–97.

5. The United States, on the other hand, had considered a preemptive strike

against the incipient Chinese nuclear weapons program. See William Burr and Jeffrey T. Richelson, "Whether to 'Strangle the Baby in the Cradle': The United States and the Chinese Nuclear Program, 1960–64," *International Security* 25, no. 3 (Winter 2000–2001): 54–99.

6. On the significance of the nuclear revolution, see Robert Jervis, *The Meaning of the Nuclear Revolution: Statecraft and the Prospect of Armageddon* (Ithaca: Cornell University Press, 1989).

7. Thomas C. Schelling, *Arms and Influence* (New Haven: Yale University Press, 1967), and Kenneth N. Waltz, *The Spread of Nuclear Weapons: More May Be Better*, Adelphi Papers 171 (London: International Institute of Strategic Studies, 1981).

8. On organizational proclivities, see Jeffrey W. Legro, *Cooperation Under Fire: Anglo-German Restraint during World War II* (Cambridge: Cambridge University Press, 1997).

9. Robert Jervis, "The Utility of Nuclear Deterrence," *International Security* 13, no. 2 (Fall 1988): 218–24.

10. John Mueller, " The Essential Irrelevance of Nuclear Weapons: Stability in the Postwar World," *International Security* 13, no. 2 (Fall 1988): 3–17.

11. Šumit Ganguly, "Wars without End? The Indo-Pakistani Conflicts," *Annals of the American Academy of Social and Political Science* (1995): 541, 167–78.

12. Sisir Gupta, *Kashmir: A Study in India-Pakistan Relations* (London: Asia Publishing House, 1966).

13. Husain Haqqani, "Partition Is History, Leave It in the Past," *India Express*, June 9, 2005.

14. Šumit Ganguly, *Conflict Unending: Indo-Pakistani Tensions since 1947* (New York: Columbia University Press, 2001).

15. Praveen Swami, *India, Pakistan, and the Secret Jihad: The Covert War in Kashmir, 1947–2004* (New York: Routledge, 2007).

16. Devin T. Hagerty, *The Consequences of Nuclear Proliferation: Lessons from South Asia* (Cambridge: MIT Press, 1998).

17. The concept of a "limited probe" is drawn from Alexander George and Richard Smoke, *Deterrence in American Foreign Policy: Theory and Practice* (New York: Columbia University Press, 1974); for an alternative argument about Pakistan's motivations underlying the Kargil probe, see Shuja Nawaz, *Crossed Swords: Pakistan, Its Army, and the Wars Within* (Karachi: Oxford University Press, 2008).

18. Šumit Ganguly and Devin T. Hagerty, *Fearful Symmetry: Indo-Pakistani Crises under the Shadow of Nuclear Weapons* (New Delhi: Oxford University Press, 2005).

19. For a discussion of both these crises, see Šumit Ganguly and R. Harrison Wagner, "India and Pakistan: Bargaining in the Shadow of Nuclear War," *Journal of Strategic Studies* 27, no. 3 (September 2004): 479–507.

20. Walter C. Ladwig III, "A Cold Start for Hot Wars? The Indian Army's New Limited War Doctrine," *International Security* 32, no. 3 (Winter 2007–8): 158–90.

21. On Pakistan's stated nuclear thresholds, see Paolo Cotta-Ramusino and Maurizio Martellini, *Nuclear Safety, Nuclear Stability, and Nuclear Strategy in Pakistan* (Como: Landau Network, 2002).

22. On the concept of "false optimism," see Steven Van Evera, *The Causes of War: Power and the Roots of Conflict* (Ithaca: Cornell University Press, 1999); on Pakistan's strategic myopia, see Ahmad Faruqui, *Rethinking the National Security of Pakistan: The Price of Strategic Myopia* (Hampshire: Ashgate, 2003).

23. On the Pakistani elite views of nuclear weapons, see Kamal Matinuddin, *The Nuclearization of South Asia* (Oxford: Oxford University Press, 2002).

24. On the likely human and economic costs of a nuclear exchange in South Asia, see Tom Shanker, "12 Million Could Die at Once in an India-Pakistan Nuclear War," *New York Times*, May 27, 2002; Bill Nichols, "Nuclear Clash Would Batter World Financial Markets," *USA Today*, June 4, 2002.

25. On the nuclear taboo, see Nina Tannenwald, *The Nuclear Taboo: The United States and the Non-use of Nuclear Weapons since 1945* (Cambridge: Cambridge University Press, 2007).

26. See Barry R. Posen, *Inadvertent Escalation* (Ithaca, N.Y.: Cornell University Press, 1991).

4. SOUTH ASIA'S NUCLEAR PAST

1. John Lewis Gaddis, *The Long Peace: Inquiries into the History of the Cold War* (New York: Oxford University Press, 1989).

2. Ashley J. Tellis, *India's Emerging Nuclear Posture* (Santa Monica, Calif.: Rand, 2001), 196–97.

3. As early as 1966, reacting to Pakistan's long-standing conventional military weakness vis-à-vis India, Pakistani prime minister Zulfikar Ali Bhutto famously promised that Pakistanis would "eat grass" if necessary to ensure their achievement of a nuclear weapons capability. However, the Bangladesh war and the Indian PNE created even stronger incentives for Paki-

stan to develop nuclear weapons. See Samina Ahmed, "Pakistan's Nuclear Weapons Program: Turning Points and Nuclear Choices," *International Security*, 32, no. 4 (Spring 1999): 183.

4. See S. Paul Kapur, *Dangerous Deterrent: Nuclear Weapons Proliferation and Conflict in South Asia* (Stanford, Calif.: Stanford University Press, 2007); Devin T. Hagerty, *The Consequences of Nuclear Proliferation: Lessons from South Asia* (Cambridge, Mass.: MIT Press, 1998).

5. A. G. Noorani, "India's Quest for a Nuclear Guarantee," *Asian Survey* 7, no. 7 (July 1967): 490–502.

6. Ashok Kapur, *India's Nuclear Option: Atomic Diplomacy and Decision-Making* (New York: Praeger, 1976).

7. Šumit Ganguly, "Why India Joined the Nuclear Club," *Bulletin of the Atomic Scientists* 39, no. 4 (April 1983): 30–33.

8. Raj Chengappa, *Weapons of Peace: The Secret Story of India's Quest to be a Nuclear Power* (New Delhi: Harper Collins, 2000).

9. Adrian Levy and Catherine Scott-Clark, *Deception: Pakistan, the United States, and the Global Nuclear Weapons Conspiracy* (New Delhi: Penguin Books, 2007).

10. Mark Tully and Satish Jacob, *Amritsar: Mrs. Gandhi's Last Battle* (London: Jonathan Cape, 1985).

11. Vivek Chadha, *Low-Intensity Conflicts in India: An Analysis* (New Delhi: Sage, 2005).

12. This was India's largest military exercise to date and comparable in size to those of the Warsaw Pact or the North Atlantic Treaty Organization in scope and dimensions. See the discussion in Šumit Ganguly, "Getting Down to Brass Tacks, *The World and I* (May 1987): 100–104.

13. Kanti Bajpai, P. R. Chari, Pervaiz Iqbal Cheema, Stephen P. Cohen, and Šumit Ganguly, *Brasstacks and Beyond: Perception and the Management of Crisis in South Asia* (New Delhi: Manohar, 1995).

14. Šumit Ganguly, *The Crisis in Kashmir: Portents of War, Hopes of Peace* (New York: Cambridge University Press, 1997).

15. On Pakistan's role in the Afghan insurgency, see Mohammed Yousaf and Mark Adkin, *Afghanistan, the Bear Trap: The Defeat of a Superpower* (Haverton: Casemate, 2001).

16. Quoted in Stanley A. Wolpert, *Zulfi Bhutto of Pakistan: His Life and Times* (New York: Oxford University Press), 194, 195, see also 191–92; Mehrunnisa Ali, "The Simla and Tashkent Agreements," in *Readings in Pakistan Foreign Policy*, ed. Mehrunnisa Ali (Karachi: Oxford University Press, 2001), 87.

17. See Sumantra Bose, *Kashmir: Roots of Conflict, Paths to Peace* (Cambridge, Mass.: Harvard University Press, 2003), 51; Šumit Ganguly, "Explaining the Kashmir Insurgency: Political Mobilization and Institutional Decay," *International Security* 21, no. 2 (Fall 1996): 80.

18. See Ahmed Rashid, *Taliban: Militant Islam, Oil, and Fundamentalism in Central Asia* (New Haven: Yale University Press, 2000), 137, 186.

19. Kapur, *Dangerous Deterrent.*

20. Interview with Benazir Bhutto, Dubai, United Arab Emirates, August 2004.

21. Interview with Shireen Mazari, Islamabad, Pakistan, April 2004; Shireen Mazari, "Kashmir: Looking for Viable Options," *Defence Journal* 3, no. 2 (February–March 1999), http://defencejournal.com/feb-mar99/kashmir-viable.htm.

22. Šumit Ganguly, *Conflict Unending: India-Pakistan Tensions since 1947* (New York: Columbia University Press, and New Delhi: Oxford University Press, 2001), 92.

23. See P. R. Chari, Pervaiz Iqbal Cheema, and Stephen Philip Cohen, *Perception, Politics, and Security in South Asia: The Compound Crisis of 1990* (London: RoutledgeCurzon, 2003), 2–4, 138.

24. This summary draws on detailed accounts of the 1990 crisis in Hagerty, *The Consequences of Nuclear Proliferation*, and Chari, Cheema, and Cohen, *Perception, Politics, and Strategy in South Asia.*

25. Mark Fineman, "Attacks Spark War Fears between India, Pakistan," *Toronto Star*, April 15, 1990, A24.

26. See Hagerty, *The Consequences of Nuclear Proliferation*, 147–48.

27. Ibid, 150–52; Chari, Cheema, and Cohen, *Perception, Politics, and Security in South Asia*, 104–14.

28. See the discussion in Michael Krepon and Mishi Faruqee, eds., "Conflict Prevention and Confidence-Building Measures in South Asia: The 1990 Crisis," Occasional Paper No. 17, Henry L. Stimson Center, Washington, D.C., April 1994.

29. Mark Fineman, "Nervous Pakistanis Watch the 'Wall' and Indian Troops," *Los Angeles Times*, April 20, 1990.

30. Salamat Ali, "Avoiding Action," *Far Eastern Economic Review* (May 3, 1990): 26.

31. P. R. Chari, *Indo-Pak Nuclear Standoff: The Role of the United States* (New Delhi: Manohar, 1995).

32. "If Pushed Beyond a Point by Pakistan, We Will Retaliate," *India Today*,

April 30, 1990, 76.

33. Beg, as quoted in Owen Bennett-Jones, *Pakistan: Eye of the Storm* (New Haven: Yale University Press, 2002), 215.

34. K. Subrahmanyam, "Capping, Managing, or Eliminating Nuclear Weapons?" in *South Asia after the Cold War*, ed. Kanti P. Bajpai and Stephen P. Cohen (Boulder: Westview Press, 1993), 184.

35. Hagerty, *The Consequences of Nuclear Proliferation*, 166.

36. Chari, Cheema, and Cohen, *Perception, Politics, and Security in South Asia*, 111.

37. Ganguly, *Conflict Unending*, 94.

38. Alexander L. George and Richard Smoke, *Deterrence in American Foreign Policy: Theory and Practice* (New York: Columbia University Press, 1974), 62, 59.

39. Hagerty, *The Consequences of Nuclear Proliferation*, 148–49.

40. Chari, Cheema, and Cohen, *Perception, Politics, and Security in South Asia*, 90–91.

41. Interview with former Indian Army chief of staff Satish Nambiar, New Delhi, India, August 2004.

42. Personal communication, S. K. Singh, January 2005.

43. Interview with Benazir Bhutto, August 2004.

44. Chari, Cheema, and Cohen, *Perception, Politics, and Security in South Asia*, 8. See also George Perkovich, *India's Nuclear Bomb: The Impact on Global Proliferation* (Berkeley and Los Angeles: University of California Press, 1999), 311.

45. The separatists had sought to establish the independent Sikh state of Khalistan. India accused Pakistan of supplying the insurgents with money and materiel, and the Pakistanis denied doing so. The issue gave rise to an Indo-Pakistani militarized standoff, known as Brasstacks, from late 1986 to early 1987.

46. See Kapur, *Dangerous Deterrent*.

47. In the twenty-five years between independence and the end of the Bangladesh conflict, India and Pakistan fought wars: in 1947–48, 1965, and 1971.

48. See V. P. Malik, *Kargil: From Surprise to Victory* (New Delhi: HarperCollins, 2006); Kargil Review Committee, *From Surprise to Reckoning* (New Delhi: Sage Publications, 2000); Amarinder Singh, *A Ridge Too Far: War in the Kargil Heights, 1999* (New Delhi: Motibagh Palace Patiala, 2001); Y. M. Bammi, *Kargil, 1999: The Impregnable Conquered* (India: Gorkha Publishers, 2002); Ashok Krishna, "The Kargil War," in *Kargil: The Tables Turned*, ed.

Ashok Krishna and P. R. Chari (New Delhi: Manohar Publishers, 2001), 77–138; Kapur, *Dangerous Deterrent*, 225n9.

49. Praveen Swami, *The Kargil War* (New Delhi: Leftword Books, 1999).
50. For a Pakistani account of the motivations underlying the Kargil conflict see Shuja Nawaz, *Crossed Swords: Pakistan, Its Army, and the Wars Within* (Karachi: Oxford University Press, 2008).
51. Ashutosh Misra, "Siachen Glacier Flashpoint: As Study of Indian-Pakistani Relations," Durham Middle East Paper No. 65, June 2000, University of Durham, Centre for Middle East and Islamic Studies.
52. Interview with senior Indian military officer, San Francisco, California, November 2000.
53. Šumit Ganguly, interviews with midlevel IAF officers, Washington, D.C., December 2000.
54. These lapses are explicitly acknowledged in the public version of the Indian government's Kargil Review Committee Report, 2000.
55. For a discussion of the nuclear danger in South Asia, see Strobe Talbott, *Engaging India: Diplomacy, Democracy, and the Bomb* (Washington, D.C.: Brookings, 2004).
56. Šumit Ganguly and Devin T. Hagerty, *Fearful Symmetry: India-Pakistan Crises in the Shadow of Nuclear Weapons* (Seattle: University of Washington Press, 2005), 161.
57. For an argument about the role of American diplomacy, see Bruce Reidel, *American Diplomacy and the 1999 Kargil Summit at Blair House* (Philadelphia: Center for the Advanced Study of India, University of Pennsylvania, 2002).
58. On the Indo-Pakistani dispute over Siachen Glacier, see V. R. Raghavan, *Siachen: Conflict without End* (New Delhi: Viking, 2002).
59. Interview with Bhutto.
60. Interview with President Pervez Musharraf, Rawalpindi, Pakistan, April 2004. Note that Musharraf maintained that local mujahideen had executed the Kargil operation, with Pakistan Army forces becoming involved only after India's counterattack had begun.
61. Interview with Jalil Jilani, Islamabad, Pakistan, April 2004. Unlike Musharraf, Jilani conceded that Pakistan Army troops had actually launched the Kargil incursions.
62. Ibid. Pakistan's nuclear capacity was not the only factor that emboldened its leaders to undertake the Kargil operation. The Pakistanis believed that retaking the Kargil heights would be prohibitively difficult for India. And

they hoped that the international community would tolerate the Kargil operation, given Pakistan's perilous position vis-à-vis a conventionally powerful, newly nuclear India. On Pakistani tactical considerations, see M. S. Qazi, "High Temperatures at High Mountains," Pakistan Institute for Air Defence Studies Home Page, http://www.piads.com.pk/users/piads/qazir.html; Sardar F. S. Lodi, "India's Kargil Operations: An Analysis," *Defence Journal* 3, no. 10 (November 1999): 2–3; Shireen Mazari, "Re-examining Kargil," *Defence Journal* 3, no. 11 (June 2000): 1, www.defencejournal.com/2000/june/reexamining.htm; Javed Nasir, "Calling the Indian Army Chief's Bluff," *Defence Journal* 3, no. 2 (February–March 1999): 25; Mirza Aslam Beg, "Kargil Withdrawal and 'Rogue' Army Image," *Defence Journal* 3, no. 8 (September 1999), http://defencejournal.com/sept99/kargil.htm; Ayaz Ahmed Khan, "Indian Offensive in the Kargil Sector," *Defence Journal* 3, no. 5 (June 1999): 7–8; Shaukat Qadir, "An Analysis of the Kargil Conflict 1999," *Royal United Service Institution Journal* 147, no. 2 (April 2002): 2–3. On international opinion see Ganguly, *Conflict Unending*, 122; Ashley J. Tellis, C. Christine Fair, and Jamison Jo Medby, *Limited Conflicts under the Nuclear Umbrella: Indian and Pakistani Lessons from the Kargil Crisis* (Santa Monica, Calif.: RAND, 2001), 38; Shireen Mazari, "Kargil: Misguided Perceptions," Pakistan Institute for Air Defence Studies, http://www.piads.com.pk/users/piads/mazarir.html; Mirza Aslam Beg, "Deterrence, Defence, and Development," *Defence Journal* 3, no. 6 (July 1999): 4–6; interview with *Friday Times* editor Ejaz Haider, Lahore, Pakistan, April 2004.

63. Interview with Mazari; Mazari, "Kashmir: Looking for Viable Options," 64; Shireen Mazari, "Low-Intensity Conflicts: The New War in South Asia," *Defence Journal* 3, no. 6 (July 1999): 41.

64. Ganguly, *Conflict Unending*, 122.

65. Ganguly and Hagerty, *Fearful Symmetry*, 191.

66. Rajesh Basrur, *Minimum Deterrence and India's Nuclear Security* (Stanford, Calif.: Stanford University Press, 2006), 73–74; Ganguly and Hagerty, *Fearful Symmetry*, 160–62.

67. Interview with former Indian Army chief of staff V. P. Malik, New Delhi, India, April 2004. On India's battle for international opinion, see also Maleeha Lodhi, "The Kargil Crisis: Anatomy of a Debacle," *Newsline* (July 1999); Tellis, Fair, and Medby, *Limited Conflicts under the Nuclear Umbrella*, 21–28; Irfan Husain, "Kargil: The Morning After," *Dawn* (Karachi) April 29, 2000.

68. Interview with G. Parthasarathy, New Delhi, India, December 2007 and August 2004.

69. Interview with Malik.

70. Interview with Brajesh Mishra, New Delhi, India, May 2005.

71. Interview with George Fernandes, New Delhi, India, August 2004.

72. Interview with A. B. Vajpayee, New Delhi, India, June 2006.

73. Interview with Malik.

74. Indian leaders' accounts here could be seen as self-serving. It would be equally advantageous, however, for the Indians to deny that they ever considered crossing the LOC during the Kargil conflict. This would enable them to claim that they were not deterred from horizontal escalation by Pakistan's nuclear capacity and would help bolster their reputation for restraint. Also note that Indian leaders do not completely dismiss the deterrent effects of Pakistani nuclear weapons; they admit to having ruled out full-scale war during Kargil because of Pakistan's nuclear capacity. Thus it is likely that if they had been similarly deterred from crossing the LOC, Indian leaders would be willing to acknowledge it.

75. See S. Paul Kapur, "Nuclear Proliferation, the Kargil Conflict, and South Asian Security," *Security Studies* 13, no. 1 (Autumn 2003): 99. Note that Lieutenant General Khalid Kidwai, director of the Pakistan Army's Strategic Plans Division, specified loss of "a large part of [Pakistani] territory" as grounds for nuclear use. See Landau Network, "Nuclear Safety, Nuclear Stability, and Nuclear Strategy in Pakistan," www.mi.infn.it/~landnet/Doc/pakistan.pdf.

76. See Tellis, Fair, and Medby, *Limited Conflicts under the Nuclear Umbrella*, x; Husain, "Kargil: The Morning After"; Zahid Husain, "On the Brink," *Newsline*, June 1999; Owen Bennett Jones, *Pakistan: Eye of the Storm* (New Haven: Yale University Press, 2002), 104; Irfan Husain, "The Cost of Kargil," *Dawn*, August 14, 1999; Husain, "Kargil: The Morning After"; Shireen M. Mazari, "Kargil: Misguided Perceptions," Pakistan Institute for Air Defence Studies, http://www.piads.com.pk/users/piads/mazari1.html; Ahmed, "Pakistan's Nuclear Weapons Program," 16; Tellis, Fair, and Medby, *Limited Conflicts under the Nuclear Umbrella*, 41, 55; "Statement of Nawaz Sharif in ATC-1," *Dawn*, March 9, 2000; Husain, "Kargil: The Morning After."

77. See Sayantan Chakravarty, "The Plot Unravels," *India Today*, December 31, 2001, 6–8.

78. For detailed discussions of the 2001–2002 crisis, see V. K. Sood and Pravin

Sawhney, *Operation Parakram: The War Unfinished* (New Delhi: Sage Publications, 2003); Polly Nayak and Michael Krepon, "U.S. Crisis Management in South Asia's Twin Peaks Crisis," Report No. 57, Henry L. Stimson Center, Washington, D.C., September 2006; Šumit Ganguly and Michael R. Kraig, "The 2001–2002 Indo-Pakistani Crisis: Exposing the Limits of Coercive Diplomacy," *Security Studies* 14, no. 2 (Summer 2005).

79. See president of Pakistan Pervez Musharraf's address to the nation, January 12, 2002, http://209.85.173.132/search?q=cache:wcLOJejbcwoJ:www.millat.com/president/1020200475758AMword%252ofile.pdf+musharraf+address+to+nation+january+12+2002&hl=en&ct=clnk&cd=1&gl=us; Alan Sipress and Rajiv Chandrasekaran, "Powell 'Encouraged' by India Visit," *Washington Post*, January 19, 2002, A19; Robert Marquand, "Powell Tiptoes Indo-Pak Divide," *Christian Science Monitor*, January 18, 2002, 6; "India-Pakistan Standoff Easing, Powell Says," *Boston Globe*, January 18, 2002, A3.

80. Interview with Mishra; Sood and Sawhney, *Operation Parakram*, 80.

81. The victims were mostly women and children, the family members of Indian military personnel. See Raj Chengappa and Shishir Gupta, "The Mood to Hit Back," *India Today*, May 27, 2002, 27–30.

82. David E. Sanger and Kurt Eichenwald, "Citing India Attack, U.S. Aims At Assets of Group in Pakistan," *New York Times*, December 21, 2001, and John F. Burns and Celia W. Dugger, "India Builds Up Forces as Bush Urges Calm," *New York Times*, December 30, 2001.

83. Celia W. Dugger, "India Raises the Pitch in Criticism of Pakistan," *New York Times*, December 19, 2001.

84. Available at www.satp.org/satporgtp/countries/pakistan/document/papers/2002Jan12.htm.

85. Celia W. Dugger, "India Welcomes Pakistani Steps, but Stays Alert," *New York Times*, January 14, 2002.

86. Todd S. Purdum, "Powell Lauds Pakistan's Efforts against Extremism," *New York Times*, January 17, 2002.

87. Šumit Ganguly and Michael R. Kraig, "The 2001–2002 Indo-Pakistani Crisis: Exposing the Limits of Coercive Diplomacy," *Security Studies* 14, no. 2 (April–June 2005): 290–324.

88. Celia W. Dugger, "Gunmen Kill 30, Including 10 children, in Kashmir," *New York Times*, May 15, 2002; Edward Luce and Farhan Bokhari, "Bombers Kill 33 in Kashmir as U.S. Envoy Visits India," *Financial Times*, May 15, 2002.

89. Edward Luce. "Back to the Brink," *Financial Times*, May 14, 2002.

90. Basharat Peer, "Vajpayee Blows Hot and Cold in Kashmir," *India Abroad*,

May 31, 2002.

91. For a discussion of India's concerns about Pakistan's nuclear capabilities, see V. Sudarshan and Ajith Pillai, "Game of Patience," *Outlook*, May 27, 2008, 35–39.

92. Praveen Swami, "A War to End a War: Causes and Outcomes of the 2001–2002 India-Pakistan Crisis," in *Nuclear Proliferation in South Asia: Crisis Behaviour and the Bomb*, ed. Šumit Ganguly and S. Paul Kapur (New York: Routledge, 2008), 144–61.

93. See, for example, Ganguly and Hagerty, *Fearful Symmetry*, 170; Basrur, *Minimum Deterrence*, 94–99.

94. Interview with Brajesh Mishra; Sood and Sawhney, *Operation Parakram*, 80.

95. Interview with V. K. Sood, New Delhi, India, August 2004.

96. Sood and Sawhney, *Operation Parakram*, 80, 82, 87; V. Sudarshan and Ajith Pillai, "Game of Patience," *Outlook* (Mumbai), May 27, 2002; interview with retired Indian generals, New Delhi, India, August 2004.

97. Interview with Vajpayee.

98. Interview with Fernandes.

99. Interview with Mishra. Note that Pakistan did not return the twenty fugitives that India had demanded.

5. SOUTH ASIA'S NUCLEAR PRESENT AND FUTURE

1. Interview with Brigadier (ret.) Gurmeet Kanwal, additional director, Centre for Land Warfare Studies, New Delhi, August 2008.

2. See Šumit Ganguly, "Will Kashmir Stop India's Rise?" *Foreign Affairs* 85, no. 4 (July–August 2006): 48; "Guns to Fall Silent on Indo-Pak Borders," *Daily Times*, November 26, 2003; "India, Pakistan Agree on Opening of New Bus Link, Trade Routes," Press Trust of India, January 18, 2006; "Indo-Pak Agreement on Reducing Risk from Accidents Relating to Nuclear Weapons—Full Text," www.hindu.com/nic/nuclear.htm; "India, Pakistan to Form Joint Group to Tackle Crime," *PakTribune*, March 23, 2006.

3. Government of India, Ministry of Home Affairs, *Annual Report, 2006–2007*, 6, 143. See also Press Trust of India, "Kashmir Violence Drops 50 Pc," October 5, 2005; Agence France Presse, "Kashmir Violence Falls to Record Low: Police," July 12, 2007; Reuters, "Kashmir Violence Falls to All-Time Low—Official," April 1, 2007.

4. Agence France Press, "Indian Troops Quit Kashmir Buildings as Violence Dips," October 31, 2007.

5. Government of India, Ministry of Home Affairs, *Annual Report, 2006–2007*, 6, 143.

6. Agence France Presse, "Kashmiri Violence Falls."

7. Interview with senior Indian diplomat, New Delhi, India, December 2007. See also Agence France Presse, "Calm in Indian Kashmir, but Pakistan Still Eyed with Suspicion," February 23, 2008.

8. Interview with managing editor of *India Today* Raj Chengappa, New Delhi, India, December 2007. See also Ganguly, "Will Kashmir Stop India's Rise?" 48–50; Robert G. Wirsing, "Precarious Partnership: Pakistan's Response to U.S. Security Policies," *Asian Affairs: An American Review* 30, no. 2 (Summer 2003): 74; Stephen Philip Cohen, "The Jihadist Threat to Pakistan," *Washington Quarterly* 26, no. 3 (Summer 2003): 14.

9. Praveen Swami, "A War to End a War: The Causes and Outcomes of the 2001–2002 India-Pakistan Crisis," in *Nuclear Proliferation in South Asia: Crisis Behaviour and the Bomb*, ed. Šumit Ganguly and S. Paul Kapur, 144–61 (London: Routledge, 2008).

10. See the discussion of the prospects and limitations of the Indian strategy of coercive diplomacy in Šumit Ganguly and Michael R. Kraig, "The 2001–2002 Indo-Pakistani Crisis: Exposing the Limits of Coercive Diplomacy," *Security Studies* 14, no. 2 (April–June 2005): 290–324.

11. Ka. S. Manjunath, Seema Sridhar, and Beryl Anand. *Indo-Pak Composite Dialogue 2000–2005: A Profile* (New Delhi: Institute of Peace and Conflict Studies, 2006).

12. For estimates of the costs of Operation Parakram for India and the commensurate costs for Pakistan, see Aditi Phadnis, "Parakram Costs Put at Rs 6,500 Crore," www.rediff.com///money/2003/jan/16defence.htm.

13. Ashley J. Tellis, "The Merits of Dehyphenation: Explaining the U.S. Success in Engaging India and Pakistan," *Washington Quarterly*, 31:4 (2008): 21–42.

14. S. Paul Kapur and Šumit Ganguly, "U.S. Should Stay out of Pakistan-India Dispute over Kashmir," *San Jose Mercury News*, December 4, 2008.

15. Axelrod refers to the "shadow of the future," the possibility of future interactions among self-interested actors as a basis for promoting cooperation in an anarchic context. See Robert Axelrod, *The Evolution of Cooperation* (New York: Basic Books, 1985).

16. On Indian doubts, based on historical experience, about the utility of

American intervention in resolving the Kashmir dispute, see Šumit Ganguly, *The Crisis in Kashmir: Portents of War, Hopes of Peace* (New York: Cambridge University Press, 1997).

17. Peter B. Evans, Harold K. Jacobson, and Robert D. Putnam, eds., *Double-Edged Diplomacy: International Bargaining and Domestic Politics* (Berkeley: University of California Press, 1993).

18. Šumit Ganguly, "The Kashmir Conundrum," *Foreign Affairs* 85, no. 4 (July–August 2006): 45–57.

19. Praveen Swami, *India, Pakistan, and the Secret Jihad: The Covert War in Kashmir, 1947–2004* (New York: Routledge, 2007).

20. Šumit Ganguly, "Political Mobilization and Institutional Decay: Explaining the Crisis in Kashmir," *International Security* 21, no. 2 (Fall 1996): 76–107.

21. Randeep Ramesh, "India Calls on UN to Ban Charity It Claims Is Front for Terror Group," *Guardian*, December 11, 2008.

22. V. R. Raghavan, "Nuclear Deterrence: An Indian Perspective," presentation at Wilton Park Conference, Steyning, West Sussex, UK, October, 12–14, 2006, www.delhipolicygroup.com/Nuclear_Deterrence_An_Indian_Perspective.htm. See also Lawrence Freedman, "Nuclear Deterrence May Still Have a Role to Play," *Financial Times*, December 1, 2006; Russell J. Leng, "Realpolitik and Learning in the India-Pakistan Rivalry," in *The India-Pakistan Conflict: An Enduring Rivalry*, ed. T. V. Paul (Cambridge: Cambridge University Press, 2005), 126–27; Swami, "A War to End a War," 144–61.

23. Pervez Musharraf, *In the Line of Fire: A Memoir* (New York: Free Press, 2006), 201–4; Stephen Philip Cohen, "The Nation and the State of Pakistan," *Washington Quarterly* 25, no. 3 (Summer 2002): 115–16; Samina Yasmeen, "Pakistan's Kashmir Policy: Voices of Moderation?" *Contemporary South Asia* 12, no. 2 (June 2003): 12; Jessie Lloyd and Nathan Nankivell, "India, Pakistan, and the Legacy of September 11," *Cambridge Review of International Affairs* 15, no. 2 (2002): 281; Wirsing, "Precarious Partnership," 71–72. Since 2002 Pakistan has received $1.9 billion in U.S. security assistance and $2.4 billion in U.S. economic aid. See Senate Committee on Foreign Relations Subcommittee on International Development, Foreign Economic Affairs and International Environmental Protection, "U.S. Foreign Assistance to Pakistan," testimony of Richard A. Boucher, assistant secretary of state for South and Central Asian affairs, December 6, 2007.

24. Yasmeen, "Pakistan's Kashmir Policy" 12, 15; Katherine Butler, "Toppling Musharraf," *Independent*, February 20, 2006. On the assassination attempts see Musharraf, *In the Line of Fire*, 244–62.

25. U.S. Department of State, "Pakistan," in Country Reports on Terrorism, 2007.

26. M. Ilyas Khan, "Pakistan Army's Tribal Quagmire," BBC News, October 9, 2007.

27. "Pakistan Welcomes New PM's Policies," BBC Monitoring, South Asia, April 1, 2008.

28. Agence France Presse, "Calm in Kashmir"; interview with Raj Chengappa.

29. Vali Nasr, "Military Rule, Islamism, and Democracy in Pakistan," *Middle East Journal* 58, no. 2 (Spring 2004): 202.

30. Jagdish Bhagwati and Padma Desai, *India: Planning for Industrialization* (London: Oxford University Press, 1970).

31. T. N. Srinivasan, *Eight Lectures on India's Economic Reforms* (New Delhi: Oxford University Press, 2000).

32. Šumit Ganguly, "India Walks a Middle Path in Gulf Conflict," *Asian Wall Street Journal Weekly*, March 4, 1991.

33. See S. Paul Kapur and Šumit Ganguly, "The Transformation of U.S.-India Relations: An Explanation for the Rapprochement and Prospects for the Future," *Asian Survey* 47, no. 4 (July–August 2007): 648–49.

34. See CIA, *World Factbook*, https://www.cia.gov/library/publications/the-world-factbook/rankorder/2001rank.html.

35. See Asian Development Bank, "South Asia's Growth to Remain Strong in 2007–2008, Says ADB," www.adb.org/Media/Articles/2007/11669-south-asian-developments-outlooks/; Asian Development Bank, "Country Reports: Key Indicators, India," www.adb.org/Documents/Books/Key_Indicators/2006/pdf/IND.pdf; Central Intelligence Agency World Factbook, "India," available at https://www.cia.gov/library/publications/the-world-factbook/geos/IN.html; K. R. Srivats, "GDP Growth Rate to be 4.8-5.5% in 2009-10," *Business Line*, March 25, 2009. The pun "Hindu growth rate" plays on the term "secular growth rate." It was coined by the Indian economist Raj Krishna.

36. World Bank, "Can South Asia End Poverty in a Generation?" web.worldbank.org/WBSITE/EXTERNAL/COUNTRIES/SOUTHASI AEXT/0,,contentMDK:21050421~pagePK:146736~piPK:146830~theSite PK:223547,00.html.

37. "India's First Priority is Spurring Economic Growth: Manmohan," Asian News International, July 9, 2008.

38. World Bank, "India Country Overview 2009," www.worldbank.org.in/ WBSITE/EXTERNAL/COUNTRIES/SOUTHASIAEXT/INDIAE

XTN/0,,contentMDK:20195738~menuPK:295591~pagePK:141137~piPK:141 127~theSitePK:295584,00.html.

39. Adil Zainulbhai, "Equitable Growth Not Just a Dream," *Financial Times* (Asia Edition), November 29, 2006.

40. Government of India, "Economic Survey, 2006–2007," http://indiabud-get.nic.in/es2006-07/esmain.htm; Jeremy Page, "India's Economy Fails to Benefit Children," *Times* (London), February 22, 2007. See also "Data and Dogma: The Great Indian Poverty Debate," *World Bank Research Observer* 20, no. 2 (Fall 2005).

41. World Bank, "India Country Overview 2009."

42. Manmohan Singh, "Opening Remarks at the 54th Meeting of the National Development Council," December 19, 2007.

43. Guy de Jonquieres, "Just Rolling Back India's State Is Not Enough," *Financial Times*, February 1, 2007; Jo Johnson, "India: Where All Is Not Yet Equal," *Financial Times*, March 14, 2007, http://www.ft.com/cms/s/0/dba09a56-ce5f-11db-b5c8-000b5df10621,dwp_uuid=d98c5ce6-ce5f-11db-b5c8-000b5df10621.html?nclick_check=1.

44. Blacksmith Institute, "The World's Worst Polluted Places," Blacksmith Institute, 2007, http://www.blacksmithinstitute.org/wwpp2007/finalReport2007.pdf.

45. Bindu Shajan Perappadan, "Air Pollution Showing Alarming Trends," *Hindu*, November 23, 2005.

46. Johnson, "India: Where All Is Not Yet Equal"; "Rs 50,000 Crore Worth Farm Produce [Going to] Waste Every Year," *Hindu*, June 20, 2005; Shalini S. Dagar, "The Missing Chain," *Business Today*, May 20, 2007; Government of India, "Economic Survey, 2006–2007."

47. Kapur and Ganguly, "The Transformation of U.S.-India Relations," 655.

48. Shivshankar Menon, "India-Pakistan: Understanding the Conflict Dynamics," speech at Jamia Millia Islamia, April 11, 2007. See also "India-Pakistan: Understanding the Conflict Dynamics," speech by Foreign Secretary Shivshankar Menon at Jamia Millia Islamia, April 11, 2007; "Pranab for Peace with Pak," *Statesman*, October 26, 2006; "Terror Threatens S. Asia: Growth Undermined and Health Care and Education Robbed of Funds, Says PM Singh," *Straights Times*, August 16, 2006.

49. See Amelia Gentleman, "Delhi Police Say Suspect Was Attack Mastermind," *International Herald Tribune*, November 13, 2005; "LeT, JeM, SIMI Helped Execute Terror Plan," *Times of India*, October 1, 2006.

50. Manmohan Singh, "PM's Statement Condemning the Blasts in Delhi,"

October 30, 2005, http://pmindia.nic.in/speeches.htm.

51. Manmohan Singh, "PM's Address to the Nation," July 12, 2006, http://pmindia.nic.in/speech/content4print.asp?id=351.

52. "Enough Is Enough," *Times of India*, October 31, 2005.

53. "Media Salute Delhi's Spirit," BBC News, October 31, 2005.

54. Manmohan Singh, "PM's Opening Remarks at the Press Conference at Mumbai," July 14, 2006, http://pmindia.nic.in/speeches.htm.

55. Interview with senior Indian diplomat closely involved with the Indo-Pakistani peace process, December 2007; interviews with senior U.S. military officials, New Delhi, India, December 2007 and May 2005; Michael Krepon, "The Meaning of the Mumbai Blasts," Henry L. Stimson Center, Washington, D.C., August 7, 2006; Walter Andersen, "The Indo-Pakistani Powder Keg," *Globe and Mail*, July 19, 2006; John H. Gill, "India and Pakistan: A Shift in the Military Calculus?" in *Strategic Asia, 2005–2006: Military Modernization in an Era of Uncertainty*, ed. Ashley J. Tellis and Michael Wills (Washington, D.C.: National Bureau of Asian Research, 2005), 266.

56. Interview with Gurmeet Kanwall, December 2007.

57. On this issue, see my discussion of India's Cold Start doctrine below.

58. The November 2008 Mumbai terror attacks occurred as this book was being completed. Available evidence indicates that Lashkar-e-Toiba was behind the operation. This would seem to be considerably more provocative than previous attacks by Pakistan-backed militants. The 2001 Parliament assault, for example, killed only a handful of people and was over in the space of a morning. The Mumbai attacks, by contrast, killed and wounded hundreds of people, continued for approximately three days, and struck India's financial nerve center, thereby threatening to undermine the country's recent economic progress. Thus far, the Manmohan Singh government has managed to resist pressures for retaliation against Pakistan. For an extended discussion of the Mumbai attacks, see chapter 6.

59. See Jane's World Defense Industry, "JWDI Briefing: India's Defence Industry," September 18, 2007; Heather Timmons and Somini Sengupta, "Building a Modern Arsenal in India," *New York Times*, August 31, 2007. See also Rodney W. Jones, "Conventional Military and Strategic Stability in South Asia," South Asian Strategic Stability Unit Research Paper No. 1, March 2005.

60. "India Rejects Pakistan's Call on Defence Budget Freeze," *Indian Express*, June 11, 2008.

61. Carin Zissis, "India's Energy Crunch," Council on Foreign Relations Back-

grounder, October 23, 2007.

62. Vibhuti Haté, "India's Energy Dilemma," South Asia Monitor, Center for Strategic and International Studies, September 7, 2006.

63. See "Booming India Steps Up Strategic Maritime Role," *Lloyd's List*, June 4, 2008, and Gurpreet Singh Khurana, "Interpreting India's Naval Strategy," *Straits Times*, July 16, 2007.

64. Interview with assistant editor of *India Today* Sundeep Unnithan, New Delhi, India, December 2007.

65. Stephen P. Cohen, *The Pakistan Army* (New Delhi: Oxford University Press, 1998), 7; Ian Talbot, *Pakistan: A Modern History* (New Delhi: Oxford University Press, 1998), 95–100.

66. See Husain Haqqani, *Pakistan: Between Mosque and Military* (Washington, D.C.: Carnegie Endowment, 2005), 14–16.

67. See International Institute for Strategic Studies, *The Military Balance, 2008* (London: Routledge, 2008), 341–46, 349–51.

68. Ashley J. Tellis, *Stability in South Asia* (Santa Monica, Calif.: Rand, 1997), 20–21; interview with Gurmeet Kanwal, director of Centre for Land Warfare Studies New Delhi, India, December 2007.

69. Interview with Unnithan, December 2007.

70. Interview with senior U.S. defense official, U.S. embassy, New Delhi, India, December 2007. For critical analyses of Parakram see, for example, V. K. Sood and Pravin Sawhney, *Operation Parakram: The War Unfinished* (New Delhi: Sage Publications, 2003); Praveen Swami, "Beating the Retreat," *Frontline*, October 26–November 8, 2002.

71. This brief overview does not purport fully to explain the complexities of India's Cold Start doctrine. It draws on the following sources: interviews in New Delhi in December 2007 with several of Cold Start's intellectual architects, including former army training command director and army vice chief of staff Vijay Oberoi; head of Center for Strategic Studies and Simulation, United Service Institution, and member of Indian National Security Council Task Force on Net Assessment and Simulation, Arun Sahgal; director of Centre for Land Warfare Studies, Gurmeet Kanwal; and senior American defense officials in New Delhi; Colonel Amarjit Singh, "Strategy and Doctrine: A Case for Convergence," presentation at Centre for Strategic Studies and Simulation, United Service Institution of India; Walter C. Ladwig III, "A Cold Start for Hot Wars? The Indian Army's New Limited War Doctrine," *International Security* 32, no. 3 (Winter 2007–8); Subhash Kapila, "India's New 'Cold Start' War Doctrine Strategically Reviewed,"

parts 1 and 2, South Asia Analysis Group Papers No. 991, May 4, 2004, and No. 1013, June 1, 2004; Tariq M. Ashraf, "Doctrinal Reawakening of the Indian Armed Forces," *Military Review* (November–December 2004): 53–62.

72. Indian planners will have to overcome a number of organizational and resource-related obstacles before they can fully implement Cold Start. See Ladwig, "A Cold Start," 1, 15–26.

73. Ashraf, "Doctrinal Reawakening," 59.

74. Interview with Oberoi. See also "Cold Start to New Doctrine," *Times of India*, April 14, 2004.

75. Interviews with Brigadier General Khawar Hanif and Major General Muhammad Mustafa Khan, Monterey, California, June 2008. See also Shaukat Qadir, "Cold Start: The Nuclear Side," *Daily Times*, May 16, 2004; and Ladwig, "A Cold Start," 10.

76. Interviews with Unnithan and senior U.S. defense official; Kapila, "India's New 'Cold Start.'"

77. Interviews with Kanwal and Sahgal.

78. Interview with senior U.S. defense official. See also Ladwig, "A Cold Start," 10–14; Gill, "India and Pakistan" 266; Cohen, "The Jihadist Threat to Pakistan," 12.

79. Benazir Bhutto's assassination is a case in point. See Mark Mazzetti, "C.I.A. Sees Qaeda Link in Death of Bhutto," *New York Times*, January 19, 2008.

80. Cited in Kanchan Lakshman, "The Expanding Jihad," *South Asia Intelligence Review* 6, no. 32 (February 18, 2008).

81. Ibid.

82. Interview with Chengappa.

83. See Yasmeen, "Pakistan's Kashmir Policy" 15; Gill, "India and Pakistan" 266; "Jihad and the State of Pakistan," *Friday Times*, March 2, 2007. See also Steve Coll, "The Stand-off: How Jihadi Groups Helped Provoke the Twenty-first Century's First Nuclear Crisis," *New Yorker*, February 13, 2006.

6. THREE POINTS OF AGREEMENT

1. See Ashley J. Tellis, "The Evolution of U.S.-Indian Ties: Missile Defense in an Emerging Strategic Relationship," *International Security* 30, no. 4 (Spring 2006): 113–51; White House, "Announcement of Withdrawal from ABM Treaty," December 13, 2001, www.whitehouse.gov/news/releas-

es/2001/12/20011213-2.html.

2. On Indian interest in Israeli and Russian capabilities, see Sanjay Badri-Maharaj, "Ballistic Missile Defense for India," www.bharat-rakshak.com/IAF/Info/BMD.html. On efforts to cooperate with the United States, see "United States Helps India Build a Missile Shield," www.foreignpolicy.com/top10-2008/index4.html.

3. Rajat Pandit, "India on Way to Joining Exclusive BMD Club," *Times of India*, November 26, 2007.

4. "Indian President Stresses Need for Missile Defense Systems," BBC Monitoring, South Asia, February 24, 2007.

5. Randeep Ramesh, "India 'Star Wars' Plan Risks New Arms Race," *Guardian*, December 14, 2007.

6. Peter J. Brown, "China Can't Stop India's Missile System," *Asia Times*, January 16, 2009.

7. Tellis, "The Evolution of U.S.-Indian Ties," 138–44.

8. Rajesh Basrur, "Missile Defense and South Asia: An Indian Perspective," in *The Impact of U.S. Ballistic Missile Defenses on Southern Asia*, ed. Michael Krepon and Chris Gagné, Report No. 46 (Washington, D.C.: Stimson Center, 2002), 18.

9. Strictly speaking, counterforce capabilities would include both counterforce nuclear weapons and ballistic missile defense. For explanatory purposes, however, we discuss counterforce nuclear weapons and BMD separately here.

10. See Charles L. Glaser, *Analyzing Strategic Nuclear Policy* (Princeton: Princeton University Press, 1990), 224; Robert Jervis, *The Illogic of American Nuclear Strategy* (Ithaca: Cornell University Press, 1984), 70. Note that, given the enormous numbers of warheads on each side, it is doubtful that either the United States or the Soviet Union could ever have acquired a significant damage limitation capacity, even with major investments in counterforce. See Glaser, *Analyzing Strategic Nuclear Policy*, 32–35; Barry R. Posen and Stephen Van Evera, "Defense Policy and the Reagan Administration: Departure from Containment," *International Security* 8, no. 1 (Summer 1983): 25–27.

11. See Robert Jervis, *The Meaning of the Nuclear Revolution: Statecraft and the Prospect of Armageddon* (Ithaca: Cornell University Press, 1989), 164–65; Glaser, *Analyzing Strategic Nuclear Policy*, 245–49; 252–54.

12. For a detailed discussion of this logic in the Cold War context, see Glaser, *Analyzing Strategic Nuclear Policy*, 116–24. For a discussion of BMD's effects

in the context of U.S. strategic relations with Russia, China, and "rogue" states, see Charles L. Glaser and Steve Fetter, "National Missile Defense and the Future of U.S. Nuclear Weapons Policy," *International Security* 26, no. 1 (Sumer 2001): 40–92.

13. Glaser, *Analyzing Strategic Nuclear Policy*, 116–24.

14. Paul Kerr and Mary Beth Nikitin, "Pakistan's Nuclear Weapons: Proliferation and Security Issues," Congressional Research Service Report for Congress, June 20, 2008, 2. India, by contrast, is estimated to have about 70 nuclear warheads. See Robert S. Norris and Hans M. Kristensen, "Indian Nuclear Forces, 2008," *Bulletin of the Atomic Scientists* (November–December 2008): 38.

15. Siddharth Srivastava, "India and the U.S. Talk Missile Defense," *Asia Times*, January 15, 2009.

16. Ramesh, "India 'Star Wars' Plan Risks New Arms Race."

17. Dinshaw Mistry, "Military Technology, National Power, and Regional Security: The Strategic Significance of India's Nuclear, Missile, Space, and Missile Defense Forces," in *South Asia's Nuclear Security Dilemma*, ed. Lowell Dittmer (New York: M. E. Sharpe, 2004), 69.

18. Robert S. Norris and Hans M. Kristensen, "Chinese Nuclear Forces, 2008," *Bulletin of the Atomic Scientists* (July–August 2008): 42.

19. See Mistry, "The Strategic Significance of India's Nuclear Forces," 68–69; Rahul Bedi, "Arms Race Fear as U.S. Plans Missile Shield in India," *Daily Telegraph*, February 28, 2008.

20. For a careful assessment of China's record on this score, see Evan S. Medeiros, *Reluctant Restraint: The Evolution of China's Nonproliferation Policies and Practices, 1980–2004* (Stanford: Stanford University Press, 2007)

21. India and Pakistan fought a bloody border war in 1962. The two countries' border disagreement remains unresolved. See Steven A. Hoffmann, *India and the China Crisis* (Berkeley: University of California Press, 1990).

22. For example, Indian policy makers were forced to go to some lengths to repair the rupture in Sino-Indian relations following the 1998 Indian nuclear tests. See John W. Garver, "The Restoration of Sino-Indian Comity Following India's Nuclear Tests," *China Quarterly* 168 (December 2001): 865–89.

23. Prachi Pinglay, "How Mumbai Attacks Unfolded," http://news.bbc.co.uk/2/low/south_asia/7757500.stm; see also Yaroslav Trofimov, Geeta Anand, Peter Wonacott, and Matthew Rosenberg, "India Security Faulted as Survivors Tell of Terror," *Wall Street Journal*, December 1, 2008.

24. James Lamont, "India Under Fire," *Financial Times*, December 2, 2008.

25. James Lamont and Farhan Bokhari, "India Calls on Pakistan to Hand Over Criminals," *Financial Times*, December 3, 2008. See also Jane Perlez and Robert F. Worth, "India Tracing Terror Attack to 2 Militants," *New York Times*, December 5, 2008, and Praveen Swami, "Mumbai Massacre Story Unfolds in Terrorist's Interrogation," *Hindu*, December 2, 2008.

26. "UNSC Bans Jamaat-ud-Dawa," *Times of India*, December 11, 2008, www.rediff.com/news/2008/dec/11mumterror-unsc-bans-jamaat-ud-dawa.htm.

27. Eric Schmitt, Mark Mazzetti, and Jane Perlez, "Pakistan's Spies Aided Group Tied to Mumbai Siege," *New York Times*, December 8, 2008.

28. Daniel Byman, *Deadly Connections: States That Sponsor Terrorism* (Cambridge: Cambridge University Press, 2005). For details concerning the ISI's involvement in Afghanistan, see Steve Coll, *Ghost Wars: The Secret History of the CIA, Afghanistan, and Bin Laden, from the Soviet Invasion to September 10, 2001* (New York: Penguin Books, 2004).

29. See S. Paul Kapur, "Ten Years of Instability in a Nuclear South Asia," *International Security* 33, no. 2 (Fall 2008): 91–92; Mark Sappenfield, "In Northwestern Pakistan, Where Militants Rule," *Christian Science Monitor*, February 28, 2008.

30. See president of Pakistan Pervez Musharraf's address to the nation, January 12, 2002, http://209.85.173.132/search?q=cache:wcLOJejbcwoJ:www.millat.com/president/1020200475758AMword%2520file.pdf+musharraf+address+to+nation+january+12+2002&hl=en&ct=clnk&cd=1&gl=us.

31. On Indian unpreparedness, see Robert F. Worth, "Lack of Preparedness Comes Brutally to Light," *New York Times*, December 4, 2008; see also Šumit Ganguly, "Delhi's Three Fatal Flaws," *Newsweek*, December 8, 2008, 19; Sudip Mazumdar, "Flunking the Intelligence Test," *Newsweek*, November 29, 2008.

32. For a discussion of possible Indian options see Siddharth Srivastava, "India Sets Sights on Pakistani Camps," *Asia Times*, December 6, 2008.

33. On the transitory features of the terrorist training camps, see Josh Meyer, "Terror Camps Scatter, Persist," *Los Angeles Times*, June 20, 2005.

34. See chapter 3 in Kapur, *Dangerous Deterrent*.

35. See chapter 6 in Kapur, *Dangerous Deterrent*

36. Note that India's Cold Start doctrine seeks to solve this problem by launching attacks serious enough to inflict significant costs on the Pakistanis, but not so threatening as to trigger a Pakistani nuclear response. It is not clear that the Indians will be able to strike this delicate balance. And, in any

event, Cold Start's implementation remains far in the future. It thus does little to address India's current problem with Pakistan-based militancy.

37. See David E. Sanger, "Strife in Pakistan Raises U.S. Doubts over Nuclear Arms," *New York Times*, May 4, 2009; Fahran Bokhari and James Lamont, "Obama Says Pakistan Nukes in Safe Hands," *Financial Times*, April 30, 2009; Kerr and Nikitin, "Pakistan's Nuclear Weapons"; Joby Warrick, "Pakistan Nuclear Security Questioned," *Washington Post*, November 11, 2007; Šumit Ganguly, "Nuclear Nonstarter," *Newsweek*, May 6, 2009, www.newsweek.com/id/195984.

38. For Pakistan's initial reaction, see Farhan Bokhari and James Lamont, "Pakistan Warns of Threat to Terror War," *Financial Times*, December 21, 2008; for subsequent reactions, see Dean Nelson, "Pakistan Blinks in India Standoff," *Times,* December 14, 2008; see also Farhan Bokhari and James Lamont, "Pakistan Battles Its Islamist Offspring," *Financial Times*, December 13/14, 2008.

39. See K. Alan Kronstadt, "Pakistan-U.S. Relations," Congressional Research Service Report for Congress, August 25, 2008, 48–51.

40. On the overhaul of the security and intelligence services, see Alan Beattie, "Security Reform Needs Singh to Change Style," *Financial Times*, December 2, 2008.

Index